# FOOD WE LOVE

FAVOURITE RECIPES FROM OUR TEST KITCHEN

THE AUSTRALIAN
**Women's Weekly**

# FOOD WE LOVE

## FAVOURITE RECIPES FROM OUR TEST KITCHEN

# contents

Thirty years ago, the now world-famous Australian Women's Weekly cookbook series was born. In 1976, we decided to compile some of the most-requested recipes from issues of The Weekly into a book that was practical and user-friendly – none of that coffee-table-book nonsense for us! No one could have predicted the results of this simple idea: the book, called *Best Ever Recipes*, was an outstanding success. Literally millions of copies were sold, and it wasn't until 2002 that we retired this revered old title.

For eight years after *Best Ever Recipes* was published, we produced just one cookbook a year, but that was not enough. As soon as a book was released, the phone in the Test Kitchen started ringing with calls from our ever-growing number of fans, asking when they could expect the next title. As *Food We Love* goes to print, we will have produced more than 140 softcover cookbooks – to say nothing of dozens of minis and larger-format books. More than 60 million copies of these books have been sold in nearly every English-speaking country in the world, and they've been translated into 11 different languages.

And it's no wonder our cookbooks are so popular. Every single recipe we publish is a fresh and original creation from our Test Kitchen. Each recipe is rigorously tested three times, each time by a different cook so we're sure everything works as it should. Our fabulous Test Kitchen staff of 16, which includes chefs, home economists, food editors and support staff, work hard to maintain our reputation for trustworthiness and reliability. We're also quick to respond to new and exciting food ideas and today, *The Australian Women's Weekly* produces a modern, fresh and exciting range of cookbooks. And to this day our Test Kitchen staff help readers who not only write and ring us, but are now also contacting us through our website and email.

A great many people have worked on our cookbooks in the Test Kitchen over the past three decades, and 90 of them have shared their most-often cooked and much-loved recipes. We think it's a fantastic selection of personal favourites from people who really care about their food, and we hope that at least some of your old favourites, maybe even some you have forgotten about, will be among those that make a wonderful return in this book.

*Pamela Clark*

Pamela Clark, Food Director

# finger food

A taste of things to come when it's love at first bite

# salmon herbed pikelets

PREPARATION TIME 20 MINUTES  COOKING TIME 15 MINUTES  MAKES 16

1 cup (150g) self-raising flour
¼ teaspoon bicarbonate of soda
⅔ cup (160ml) buttermilk
1 egg, beaten lightly
15g butter, melted
2 tablespoons coarsely chopped fresh flat-leaf parsley
2 tablespoons finely chopped fresh chives

### SALMON TOPPING
185g packaged cream cheese
1 tablespoon lemon juice
210g can red salmon, drained

1 Sift flour and soda into medium bowl, stir in combined buttermilk, egg, butter, parsley and half of the chives; mix to a smooth batter (or process until smooth).
2 Drop tablespoons of batter into hot oiled frying pan. Cook one side until browned lightly; turn, cook other side. Cool on wire rack.
3 Meanwhile, blend or process ingredients for salmon topping until smooth.
4 Spoon topping onto pikelets; sprinkle with remaining chives.
   **per pikelet**  6.6g total fat (3.6g saturated fat); 456kJ (109 cal); 7.1g carbohydrate; 5.3g protein; 0.4g fibre

"If someone asks me to bring a plate, these jump immediately to mind. The salmon topping can be made the day before, and it's also great simply eaten with french bread."

Denise Henkel
spent five years in the Test Kitchen in the late '60s before moving to Germany. She now lives on the NSW south coast with her husband and has three children and five grandchildren.

# creamy smoked salmon tartlets

**PREPARATION TIME** 15 MINUTES  **COOKING TIME** 30 MINUTES  **MAKES** 24

3 sheets ready-rolled puff pastry

100g smoked salmon, chopped finely

2 gherkins, chopped finely

2 green onions, chopped finely

½ cup (120g) sour cream

1 tablespoon milk

2 eggs, beaten lightly

1 teaspoon finely chopped fresh dill

¼ teaspoon hot paprika

1 Preheat oven to moderate (180°C/160°C fan-forced). Lightly grease 12-hole shallow patty pan.

2 Cut 24 x 6.5cm rounds from pastry; place into patty pan holes.

3 Sprinkle salmon, gherkin and onion into pastry cases; pour in combined sour cream, milk, egg, dill and paprika. Bake about 30 minutes. Serve hot.

**per tartlet**  7.4g total fat (1.8g saturated fat); 464kJ (111 cal); 8.4g carbohydrate; 2.9g protein; 0.4g fibre

"Everyone seems to love these no matter what age they are... even my five-year-old asks for more!"

Kathy Knudsen (nee Wharton) is a trained chef who worked in the Test Kitchen for six years, three of those as a senior home economist. Now working freelance, Kathy has three small children who keep her extremely busy.

# thai coconut prawns

PREPARATION TIME 30 MINUTES  COOKING TIME 15 MINUTES  MAKES 24

24 uncooked medium prawns (1kg)
¼ cup (35g) plain flour
2 eggs, beaten lightly
1½ cups (115g) shredded coconut
½ cup (125ml) sweet chilli sauce
2 tablespoons water
2 tablespoons coarsely chopped fresh coriander

1 Preheat oven to moderate (180°C/160°C fan-forced). Lightly oil two oven trays.
2 Shell and devein prawns. Coat prawns in flour, shake away excess; dip into egg, then coat in coconut.
3 Thread one prawn on each skewer; place, in single layer, on trays. Bake, uncovered, about 15 minutes or until prawns are cooked through.
4 Meanwhile, combine remaining ingredients in small bowl to make dipping sauce.
5 Serve hot prawns with dipping sauce.

tips Prawns can be skewered and dipping sauce made a day ahead. Keep; covered, in refrigerator.

You need 24 bamboo skewers; soak them in cold water for at least an hour prior to use to prevent them from splintering and scorching.

per prawn 3.7 total fat (2.8g saturated fat); 268kJ (64 cal); 2.4g carbohydrate; 5.3g protein; 1g fibre

"My friends are always impressed with these prawns, and the best part is that they're easy and fast to prepare."

Kellie McChesney (nee Ann) spent 2001 and 2002 in the Test Kitchen, half of that time as senior home economist. She now works with a partner in their new Sydney-based food product business.

# vietnamese rice-paper rolls

PREPARATION TIME 45 MINUTES (PLUS REFRIGERATION TIME)  COOKING TIME 10 MINUTES
MAKES 24

80g bean thread noodles
1 tablespoon peanut oil
600g chicken breast fillets
⅓ cup (80ml) peanut oil, extra
1 teaspoon sesame oil
⅓ cup (80ml) mirin
2 tablespoons finely chopped fresh lemon grass
2 teaspoons fish sauce
2 teaspoons kecap manis
4cm piece fresh ginger (20g), chopped finely
2 cloves garlic, crushed
½ cup finely shredded fresh mint
1 small red onion (100g), sliced finely
½ cup (75g) roasted unsalted cashews, chopped finely
1 cup (80g) bean sprouts
2 tablespoons finely grated lime rind
4 fresh small red thai chillies, chopped finely
24 x 21cm-round rice-paper sheets
24 fresh mint leaves

### DIPPING SAUCE
½ cup (125ml) mirin
¼ cup (60ml) kecap manis
⅓ cup (80ml) lime juice

"I love these rice-paper rolls because they have a fresh flavour, use healthy ingredients and can be made ahead of time – a real bonus."

Kathy McGarry worked full-time in the Test Kitchen from 1990 until the end of 1996... and she still remembers it as "an awesome job!". She now lives on the Gold Coast, with her young family.

1 Place noodles in medium heatproof bowl, cover with boiling water; stand until just tender, drain. Cut into 4cm lengths.

2 Heat peanut oil in medium frying pan; cook chicken until browned both sides and cooked through. Cut chicken into thin slices.

3 Combine extra peanut oil, sesame oil, mirin, lemon grass, sauce, kecap manis, ginger, garlic and shredded mint in large bowl; stir in noodles, chicken, onion, cashews, sprouts, rind and chilli. Cover; refrigerate 30 minutes.

4 Meanwhile, combine ingredients for dipping sauce in small bowl.

5 Place 1 sheet of rice paper in medium bowl of warm water until just softened; lift from water carefully, place on board. Place 1 mint leaf in centre of rice paper; top with 1 heaped tablespoon of filling. Roll to enclose, folding in ends (roll should be about 8cm long). Repeat with remaining rice-paper sheets, mint and filling.

6 Serve rolls with dipping sauce.

tip  Dipping sauce can be made two days ahead. Rolls can be made three hours ahead; keep, covered, in refrigerator.

per roll  6.3g total fat (1.2g saturated fat); 489kJ (117 cal); 6.6g carbohydrate; 6.6g protein; 0.8g fibre

# figs with prosciutto

PREPARATION TIME 5 MINUTES  MAKES 12

6 large black figs (480g), halved
6 slices prosciutto (90g), halved
3 teaspoons balsamic vinegar

1 Arrange figs on serving platter, top with prosciutto. Drizzle figs with
vinegar and sprinkle with pepper.
**tip**  Recipe is best made just before serving.
**per fig**  0.5g total fat (0.2g saturated fat); 100kJ (24 cal); 3g carbohydrate;
1.9g protein; 0.9g fibre

"This reminds me
of long summer
lunches in the south
of France, always
followed by a big
globe artichoke and
washed down with
lots of rosé."

Kellie-Marie Thomas
was born in WA, lived in
Wales until she was 10 when
she moved to Bahrain, did a
degree in Brighton, England,
and is now a senior home
economist in the Test Kitchen.

"These are great for entertaining – they can be prepared to the cooking stage well in advance, and they're so tasty, no one is able to stop at just a couple!"

Karen Green
worked in several different positions in the Test Kitchen during the late '80s and early '90s, latterly as assistant food editor and finally freelancer.

# gorgonzola fritters

PREPARATION TIME 15 MINUTES (PLUS STANDING TIME)  COOKING TIME 15 MINUTES  MAKES 36

1 cup (200g) ricotta
1 cup (185g) coarsely chopped gorgonzola
2 eggs, beaten lightly
½ cup (75g) plain flour
vegetable oil, for deep-frying
1 cup (80g) finely grated parmesan

1 Combine ricotta, gorgonzola and egg in medium bowl. Whisk in flour; stand 1 hour.
2 Heat oil in a large saucepan; deep-fry heaped teaspoons of cheese mixture, turning occasionally, until fritters are browned lightly all over and cooked through. (Do not have oil too hot or fritters will over-brown before cooking through.)
3 Place parmesan in medium bowl; toss hot fritters, in batches, to coat as they are cooked.

tip Gorgonzola is a creamy, blue cheese from Italy; if unavailable, use blue castello or a similar soft blue cheese.

per fritter 3.9g total fat (2.1g saturated fat); 226kJ (54 cal); 1.6g carbohydrate; 3.1g protein; 0.1g fibre

# zucchini, leek and fetta frittata

**PREPARATION TIME** 15 MINUTES  **COOKING TIME** 50 MINUTES (PLUS COOLING TIME)  **MAKES** 25

1 tablespoon olive oil

20g butter

2 medium zucchini (240g), grated coarsely

2 small leeks (400g), sliced thinly

1 clove garlic, crushed

8 eggs, beaten lightly

½ cup (125ml) cream

100g fetta, crumbled

½ cup (40g) finely grated parmesan

2 tablespoons finely chopped fresh mint

2 tablespoons polenta

2 tablespoons finely grated parmesan, extra

50g fetta, crumbled, extra

1 Preheat oven to moderate (180°C/160°C fan-forced). Grease 23cm-square slab pan; line base and two sides with baking paper, extending paper 2cm above edges.

2 Heat oil and butter in large frying pan, add zucchini, leek and garlic; cook, stirring, until leek is soft. Transfer to medium bowl; cool.

3 Add egg, cream, cheeses and mint to bowl, stir to combine; pour into pan. Sprinkle with combined polenta and extra cheeses.

4 Bake about 40 minutes or until set. Cool in pan.

5 Cut frittata into 25 pieces.

**tip** Frittata can be made a day ahead; keep, covered, in refrigerator.

**per frittata** 7.4.g total fat (3.9g saturated fat); 376kJ (90 cal); 1.4g carbohydrate; 4.5g protein; 0.5g fibre

"A favourite of my family and friends, this dish is delicious served hot or cold, making it good picnic or buffet fare."

Karen Buckley has been involved professionally in the cooking industry for almost 20 years, demonstrating and developing recipes, and teaching evening classes at a local college.

# mini beef and guinness pies

PREPARATION TIME 20 MINUTES  COOKING TIME 1 HOUR 50 MINUTES (PLUS REFRIGERATION TIME)
MAKES 36

1 tablespoon vegetable oil
500g beef skirt steak, chopped finely
1 medium brown onion (150g), chopped finely
2 tablespoons plain flour
375ml bottle guinness stout
1 cup (250ml) beef stock
5 sheets ready-rolled shortcrust pastry
1 egg, beaten lightly

1 Heat oil in large saucepan, add beef; cook, stirring, until browned. Add onion; cook, stirring, until softened. Add flour; cook, stirring, until mixture bubbles and is well browned.

2 Gradually add stout and stock, stirring until gravy boils and thickens. Cover, reduce heat; simmer, stirring occasionally, 1 hour. Uncover; simmer, stirring occasionally, 30 minutes. Cool filling 10 minutes then refrigerate until cold.

3 Preheat oven to hot (220°C/200°C fan-forced). Lightly grease three 12-hole mini (1 tablespoon/20ml) muffin pans.

4 Using 6cm pastry cutter, cut 36 rounds from pastry sheets; place 1 round in each of the muffin pan holes. Using 5cm pastry cutter, cut 36 rounds from remaining pastry sheets.

5 Spoon 1 heaped teaspoon of the cold filling into each pastry case; brush around edges with beaten egg. Top each pie with smaller pastry round, press gently around edge to seal; brush with remaining egg. Using sharp knife, make two small slits in top of each pie.

6 Bake pies about 15 minutes or until browned lightly. Stand 5 minutes in pan before placing on serving platters.

tip  Cooked pies can be frozen for up to two months.

per pie  7.4g total fat (3.6g saturated fat); 564kJ (135 cal); 11.3g carbohydrate; 5.1g protein; 0.5g fibre

# cheese and olive loaf

**PREPARATION TIME** 15 MINUTES  **COOKING TIME** 35 MINUTES  **SERVES** 6

1 cup (150g) self-raising flour

⅔ cup (50g) coarsely grated parmesan

2 tablespoons coarsely chopped fresh mint

½ teaspoon ground black pepper

1 cup (120g) seeded black olives, chopped coarsely

75g mortadella, chopped coarsely

4 eggs, beaten lightly

80g butter, melted

1 Preheat oven to moderately hot (200°C/180°C fan-forced). Lightly grease 8cm x 26cm bar cake pan.

2 Sift flour into medium bowl, add cheese, mint, pepper, olives and mortadella.

3 Add egg and butter; stir until well combined. Spread mixture into pan; bake about 35 minutes or until browned lightly. Turn onto wire rack to cool.

**tips** Recipe can be made a day ahead; keep, covered, in refrigerator. Loaf suitable to freeze.

**per serving** 21.3g total fat (11.2g saturated fat); 1371kJ (328 cal); 22.5g carbohydrate; 12.1g protein; 1.5g fibre

"This was based on an old recipe of my mother's that called for a bit of this and a pinch of that. I updated it for the WW's *Easy Greek-style cookery* book and now make it for my two girls' lunchboxes."

Dimitra Alfred (nee Stais) spent years reading the WW's food pages, so working in the Test Kitchen in the early '90s was a dream job. It fostered a passion for food that took her to Europe where she researched the food and recipes of her Greek heritage.

# sausage rolls

PREPARATION TIME 25 MINUTES  COOKING TIME 25 MINUTES  MAKES 48

4 sheets ready-rolled puff pastry

1 egg, beaten lightly

FILLING

750g sausage mince

1 medium white onion (150g), chopped finely

1 cup (70g) stale breadcrumbs

1 teaspoon dried mixed herbs

1 egg, beaten lightly

1 Preheat oven to moderately hot (200°C/180°C fan-forced). Grease two oven trays.

2 Combine filling ingredients in large bowl. Cut each sheet of pastry in half.

3 Spoon filling into piping bag. Pipe filling along one long side of each pastry sheet. Brush opposite edge of pastry with egg; roll up pastry from filled edge to enclose filling. Cut into 6 even pieces, place on trays. Brush with egg; cut small slits in top of each roll. Bake about 25 minutes or until well browned.

tips  Sausage rolls can be frozen, cooked or uncooked, for two months. Reheat frozen cooked sausage rolls in moderate oven about 25 minutes, or cook frozen uncooked sausage rolls in moderate oven about 45 minutes.

per sausage roll  7.1g total fat (1.9g saturated fat); 426kJ (102 cal); 6.6g carbohydrate; 3.1g protein; 0.6g fibre

"Whenever I have a party, these are always the first to go. People are forever commenting on how great and tasty they are."

Elizabeth Hooper worked in the Test Kitchen for 13 years, the last few of which were spent as Test Kitchen manager. She left in 2001 to pursue study and embark on a career change.

# soups & starters

A great beginning signals a memorable meal

soups

# speedy minestrone

PREPARATION TIME 10 MINUTES  COOKING TIME 40 MINUTES  SERVES 6

30g butter
1 medium brown onion (150g), sliced thinly
1 clove garlic, crushed
2 bacon rashers (140g), chopped coarsely
1 trimmed celery stalk (100g), chopped coarsely
1 medium carrot (120g), chopped coarsely
400g can chopped tomatoes
310g can red kidney beans, rinsed, drained
3 cups (750ml) chicken stock
⅓ cup spiral pasta
¼ cup (20g) flaked parmesan
2 tablespoons finely chopped fresh flat-leaf parsley

1 Heat butter in large saucepan, add onion, garlic and bacon; stir over medium heat until onion is soft. Add celery and carrot; stir over heat 2 minutes.

2 Stir in undrained tomatoes, beans, stock and pasta. Bring to a boil, reduce heat; simmer, covered, 30 minutes. Serve topped with cheese and parsley.

**tips** Minestrone can be made up to two days ahead; keep, covered, in refrigerator, or freeze for up to two months.

**per serving** 7.9g total fat (4.3g saturated fat); 752kJ (180 cal); 17.6g carbohydrate; 9.6g protein; 4.6g fibre

"This is a really easy, delicious soup that can be ready in less than an hour. Great on a cold day."

Jane Ash (nee Cleary) worked in the Test Kitchen from 1986 to 1990 and has kept in touch. After an eight-year stint as a hospitality teacher, she became cookery editor for *Take 5*. She is mother to two teenagers and an eight-year-old.

# wintry lamb and vegetable soup

**PREPARATION TIME** 20 MINUTES **COOKING TIME** 1 HOUR 45 MINUTES **SERVES** 4

4 lamb shanks (1kg)

2 medium carrots (240g), chopped coarsely

2 medium white onions (300g), chopped coarsely

2 cloves garlic, crushed

2 medium potatoes (400g), chopped coarsely

2 trimmed celery stalks (200g), chopped coarsely

400g can chopped tomatoes

1.5 litres (6 cups) beef or chicken stock

½ cup (125ml) tomato paste

2 medium zucchini (240g), chopped coarsely

1 Combine lamb, carrot, onion, garlic, potato, celery, undrained tomatoes, stock and paste in large saucepan. Bring to a boil, reduce heat; simmer, covered, 1 hour.

2 Add zucchini, simmer, uncovered, further 30 minutes or until lamb is tender.

3 Remove lamb from soup. When cool enough to handle, remove meat from bones, discard bones. Return meat to soup, stir until heated through.

**tip** Recipe can be made three days ahead; keep, covered, in refrigerator.

**per serving** 9.2g total fat (3.9g saturated fat); 1513kJ (362 cal); 29.2g carbohydrate; 39.7g protein; 8.5g fibre

"This soup is made without fail every winter; it's a great family meal, and I have served it at dinner parties."

Tracey Port (nee Kern) joined our Test Kitchen for three years, then freelanced in recipe development and cooking for photography. In 1999, after having two sons, she started a cake decorating business.

# pho bo

**PREPARATION TIME** 40 MINUTES  **COOKING TIME** 2 HOURS 30 MINUTES  **SERVES** 6

Pronounced "fah bah", this Vietnamese beef noodle soup has assumed cult status in the past decade or so, with restaurants specialising in it opening up throughout the western world. Many places serve the beef raw, allowing diners to drop it, piece by piece, into the hot broth to cook at the table.

1.5kg beef bones
2 medium brown onions (300g), chopped coarsely
2 medium carrots (240g), chopped coarsely
4 trimmed celery stalks (400g), chopped coarsely
2 cinnamon sticks
4 star anise
6 cardamom pods, bruised
10 black peppercorns
2 tablespoons fish sauce
6 cloves
12cm piece fresh ginger (60g), sliced thinly
6 cloves garlic, sliced thinly
500g piece gravy beef
4 litres (16 cups) water
2 tablespoons soy sauce
200g bean thread vermicelli
½ cup loosely packed fresh vietnamese mint leaves
4 fresh small red thai chillies, sliced thinly
1 medium brown onion (150g), sliced thinly, extra
½ cup loosely packed fresh coriander leaves
1¼ cups (100g) bean sprouts

1  Preheat oven to hot (220°C/200°C fan-forced).
2  Combine beef bones, onion, carrot and celery in large baking dish; roast, uncovered, about 45 minutes or until browned all over. Drain excess fat from dish.
3  Combine beef mixture, cinnamon, star anise, cardamom, peppercorns, fish sauce, cloves, ginger, garlic, gravy beef and the water in large saucepan. Bring to a boil; simmer, uncovered, 1½ hours, skimming occasionally. Strain through muslin-lined strainer into large bowl. Reserve broth and beef; discard bones and spices. When beef is cool enough to handle, shred finely; return with soy sauce and broth to cleaned pan.
4  Just before serving, place vermicelli in large heatproof bowl; cover with boiling water, stand 3 minutes, drain.
5  Divide vermicelli among serving bowls; top with broth and beef mixture, mint, chilli, extra onion and coriander. Serve with sprouts.

**tip** Chicken can be substituted for the beef, if preferred.

**per serving**  4.7g total fat (1.9g saturated fat); 1074kJ (257 cal); 30.1g carbohydrate; 23g protein; 6.2g fibre

"I love this light but filling soup; it brings back memories of many a 'group' lunch at the Test Kitchen."

Amanda Lennon (nee Kelly) worked at the Test Kitchen for four years, after which she took on the role of food editor for a food magazine for four years, and then became a senior food editor of a dieting magazine.

"My dad loved this recipe, it was great sitting around with my family, eating and dipping crusty bread in the sauce."

Ariarne Bradshaw was a chef for 13 years before arriving in the Test Kitchen. She is now a home economist working on the WW cookbooks.

# bouillabaisse

PREPARATION TIME 45 MINUTES   COOKING TIME 40 MINUTES   SERVES 6

6 uncooked small blue swimmer crabs (2kg)

2 tablespoons olive oil

4 cloves garlic, crushed

2 medium white onions (300g), chopped finely

¼ cup (70g) tomato paste

¾ cup (180ml) dry white wine

2 x 400g cans chopped tomatoes

½ teaspoon ground turmeric

2 bay leaves

2 teaspoons white sugar

1½ cups (375ml) water

1kg firm white fish fillets, chopped coarsely

500g uncooked large prawns

250g scallops

250g calamari rings

1 Remove and discard triangular flap from underside of each crab. Remove and discard the whitish gills, liver and brain matter; rinse crab well. Crack nippers slightly; chop down centre of each crab to separate body into 2 pieces.

2 Heat oil in large saucepan, add garlic and onion; cook, stirring, until onion is soft.

3 Stir in tomato paste, wine, undrained tomatoes, turmeric, bay leaves, sugar and the water. Bring to a boil, reduce heat, simmer, uncovered, 10 minutes.

4 Add crab and fish to tomato mixture, bring to a boil; reduce heat, simmer, covered, 5 minutes.

5 Meanwhile, shell and devein prawns leaving tails intact. Remove vein from scallops.

6 Stir prawns, scallops and calamari into tomato mixture, bring to a boil, reduce heat, simmer until prawns just change colour.

7 Serve bouillabaisse immediately, with fresh crusty bread, if desired.

tips Recipe must be made and served immediately, as seafood does not reheat successfully.

You will need to use an extra large saucepan to fit in all the seafood.

per serving 11.7g total fat (2.4g saturated fat); 1843kJ (441 cal); 11.3g carbohydrate; 67.2g protein; 3.1g fibre

## starters

# salt and pepper prawns

PREPARATION TIME 20 MINUTES  COOKING TIME 5 MINUTES  SERVES 6

18 uncooked large prawns (1.2kg)
2 teaspoons sea salt
¼ teaspoon five-spice powder
½ teaspoon freshly ground black pepper

1 Shell and devein prawns leaving tails intact. Thread each of the prawns onto a skewer lengthways.
2 Combine remaining ingredients in small bowl.
3 Cook prawn skewers on heated oiled barbecue (or grill or grill plate) over high heat until browned both sides and just cooked through. Sprinkle with half the salt mixture during cooking.
4 Serve prawn skewers with remaining salt mixture.

**tips** You will need to soak the skewers in water for up to one hour before using to prevent them scorching and splintering.
Prawns can be peeled and skewered up to six hours ahead. Barbecue just before serving.

**per serving**  0.5g total fat (0.1g saturated fat); 309kJ (74 cal); 0.0g carbohydrate; 17.1g protein; 0.0g fibre

"These look and taste fabulous. I love this recipe because it has the 'wow' factor. It can be served as part of a casual seafood barbecue or as finger food for a cocktail party."

Frances Abdallaoui is the WW's deputy food editor. She joined the magazine in 1999, after being part of the 1993 to 1994 Test Kitchen team. Fran is married with two children.

# mustard-seed chilli prawns

PREPARATION TIME 20 MINUTES  COOKING TIME 7 MINUTES  SERVES 4

Mustard seeds are available in black, brown or yellow varieties; here, we used black, as they are more spicy and piquant than the other varieties. You can purchase mustard seeds from major supermarkets or health-food shops.

1kg uncooked large prawns
¼ teaspoon ground turmeric
2 fresh small red thai chillies, chopped finely
2 tablespoons vegetable oil
2 teaspoons black mustard seeds
2 cloves garlic, crushed
2 tablespoons finely chopped fresh coriander

1 Shell and devein prawns, leaving tails intact. Cut along backs of prawns, taking care not to cut all the way through; flatten prawns slightly.
2 Rub turmeric and chilli into prawns in medium bowl.
3 Heat oil in large frying pan; cook mustard seeds and garlic, stirring, until seeds start to pop. Add prawns; cook, stirring, until prawns just change colour. Stir in coriander.
   **tip** If you like hot dishes, don't seed the chillies before chopping, as removing the seeds and membranes lessens the heat level.
   **per serving**  10g total fat (1.3g saturated fat); 811kJ (194 cal); 0.2g carbohydrate; 25.8g protein; 0.3g fibre

# vodka-cured gravlax

**PREPARATION TIME** 10 MINUTES (PLUS REFRIGERATION TIME) **MAKES** 24

1 tablespoon sea salt

1 teaspoon ground black pepper

1 tablespoon white sugar

1 tablespoon vodka

300g salmon fillet, skin on

24 melba toasts

### SOUR CREAM SAUCE

⅓ cup (80g) sour cream

2 teaspoons drained baby capers, rinsed

2 teaspoons lemon juice

2 teaspoons finely chopped drained cornichons

½ small red onion (50g), chopped finely

1 Combine salt, pepper, sugar and vodka in small bowl.

2 Remove bones from fish; place fish, skin-side down, on piece of plastic wrap. Spread vodka mixture over flesh side of fish; enclose securely in plastic wrap. Refrigerate overnight, turning parcel several times.

3 Combine ingredients for sour cream sauce in small bowl.

4 Slice fish thinly; spread sauce on toasts, top with fish.

**per piece** 2.4g total fat (1.1g saturated fat); 230kJ (55 cal); 4.7g carbohydrate; 3.2g protein; 0.3g fibre

"I love making this; whenever I have a chance, I make it at dinners and cocktail parties. Everyone always loves it."

Susie Riggall graduated from university and turned to finance before cooking excited her interest. After a year in the Test Kitchen, she left to pursue a career as a personal chef.

# potato terrine

PREPARATION TIME 1 HOUR  COOKING TIME 2 HOURS AND 15 MINUTES (PLUS STANDING TIME)
SERVES 8

2 large potatoes (600g)
1 medium red capsicum (200g)
1 large eggplant (500g)
cooking-oil spray
1 large leek (500g)
⅓ cup (80ml) olive oil
3 cloves garlic, crushed
2 tablespoons finely chopped fresh thyme
1 teaspoon ground black pepper
10 slices (150g) prosciutto
250g mozzarella, sliced
1 cup loosely packed fresh basil leaves

### SAFFRON VINAIGRETTE
⅓ cup (80ml) olive oil
2 tablespoons lemon juice
pinch saffron threads

1  Preheat oven to moderate (180°C/160°C fan-forced). Grease 14cm x 21cm loaf pan.
2  Cut potatoes into 2mm slices. Add potato to large saucepan of boiling water; cook about 4 minutes or until potatoes are just beginning to soften; drain.
3  Quarter capsicum, remove seeds and membranes. Roast under preheated grill, skin-side up, until skin blisters and blackens. Cover capsicum pieces in plastic or paper 5 minutes; peel away skin.
4  Cut eggplant lengthways into 5mm slices; spray slices, both sides, with oil. Cook eggplant, in large frying pan, until browned both sides; drain on absorbent paper.
5  Cut white part of leek into 7cm lengths; cut lengths in half. Boil, steam or microwave leek until tender. Drain, rinse under cold water; drain.
6  Combine oil, garlic, thyme and pepper in small bowl.
7  Cover base and long sides of pan with prosciutto, allowing prosciutto to overhang edges. Place half of the potato, overlapping, over base, brush with herb oil mixture; top with half of the cheese, brush with herb oil mixture. Layer capsicum, eggplant, basil and leek, brushing each layer with herb oil mixture. Top leek layer with remaining cheese then remaining potato, brushing with herb oil mixture between layers; press down firmly. Cover terrine with prosciutto slices.
8  Cover terrine with foil, place on oven tray. Cook 1 hour; uncover, cook further 40 minutes. Remove from oven, pour off any liquid. Cool 5 minutes; cover top of terrine with plastic wrap, weight with two large heavy cans for 1 hour.
9  Combine ingredients for saffron vinaigrette in jar; shake well. Serve with sliced terrine.

**tip** Terrine is best made a day ahead; keep, covered, in refrigerator.

**per serving** 27.1g total fat (7.4g saturated fat); 1476kJ (353 cal); 12.8g carbohydrate; 15.1g protein; 4.3g fibre

"It takes a little extra effort to make, but gives great satisfaction – it presents so well and tastes delicious."

Tora Tarlinton arrived in Australia from Norway in 1968 and, almost immediately, secured a job in the Test Kitchen; then, four years later, opened her own catering business. She has now retired to Queensland.

# tuna tartare with avocado salsa and parmesan crisps

PREPARATION TIME 40 MINUTES  COOKING TIME 5 MINUTES  SERVES 4

1 cup (80g) coarsely grated parmesan
½ fresh long red chilli, sliced thinly
400g piece sashimi tuna, trimmed
1 small avocado (200g), chopped finely
3 small tomatoes (270g), seeded, chopped finely
1 small red onion (100g), chopped finely
⅓ cup loosely packed fresh coriander leaves

### CHILLI LIME DRESSING

½ fresh long red chilli, sliced thinly
1 teaspoon finely grated lime rind
⅓ cup (80ml) lime juice
1 clove garlic, crushed
2 teaspoons finely chopped coriander root and stem
2 tablespoons olive oil

1 Preheat oven to hot (220°C/200°C fan-forced).

2 Combine cheese and chilli in small bowl. Drop level tablespoons of the cheese mixture on baking-paper-lined oven tray, flattening slightly with back of spoon. Bake, uncovered, about 5 minutes or until browned lightly. Stand until parmesan crisps set.

3 Meanwhile, place ingredients for chilli lime dressing in screw-top jar; shake well.

4 Cut tuna into 5mm pieces. Place in medium bowl with half of the dressing; toss gently.

5 Place avocado, tomato, onion and coriander in medium bowl with remaining dressing; toss gently to combine salsa.

6 Press a quarter of the undrained tuna into a 9cm egg ring set on serving plate; remove egg ring, top tuna with a quarter of the salsa. Repeat with remaining tuna and salsa; serve tartare with parmesan crisps.

tip Tuna sold as sashimi has to meet stringent guidelines regarding its handling and treatment after leaving the water. Regardless, it is still probably a good idea to know your fishmonger quite well, or to seek advice from local authorities before eating any raw seafood.

per serving 29.3g total fat (9.4g saturated fat); 1722kJ (412 cal); 2.5g carbohydrate; 34.3g protein; 1.5g fibre

"Fish is my specialty. Here's one recipe that shows off the beauty of raw tuna. It's great for a dinner party."

Nancy Duran turned from advertising in her native US to become a chef in top restaurants in Sydney and New York. She joined the Test Kitchen team in 2003 before leaving in 2004 to become an assistant food editor on a food magazine.

# laila's lamb kofta with spiced yogurt

**PREPARATION TIME** 30 MINUTES (PLUS REFRIGERATION TIME) **COOKING TIME** 20 MINUTES
**MAKES** 40

¼ cup (40g) burghul
500g lamb mince
1 egg, beaten lightly
1 medium brown onion (150g), chopped finely
¼ cup (40g) pine nuts, chopped finely
2 tablespoons finely chopped fresh mint
2 tablespoons finely chopped fresh flat-leaf parsley
vegetable oil, for shallow-frying

### SPICED YOGURT

2 small red thai chillies, chopped finely
1 tablespoon finely chopped fresh mint
1 tablespoon finely chopped fresh flat-leaf parsley
1 tablespoon finely chopped fresh coriander
1 clove garlic, crushed
½ teaspoon ground cumin
500g thick yogurt

> "This is my mum's special kofta recipe, which she makes every Christmas and Easter."
>
> Amira Georgy (nee Ibram) has degrees in journalism and Japanese. A food lover, she interviewed Pamela Clark then said, "I want a job here!" After four years as assistant food editor on the Test Kitchen cookbooks, Amira joined the editorial team of a food and lifestyle magazine.

1 Cover burghul with cold water in small bowl; stand 10 minutes. Drain; pat dry with absorbent paper to remove as much water as possible.

2 Using one hand, combine burghul in large bowl with lamb, egg, onion, nuts and herbs. Roll rounded teaspoons of the lamb mixture into kofta balls. Place on tray, cover; refrigerate 30 minutes.

3 Heat oil in large frying pan; shallow-fry kofta, in batches, until browned all over and cooked through. Drain on absorbent paper.

4 Meanwhile, combine ingredients for spiced yogurt in medium bowl.

5 Serve kofta hot with spiced yogurt.

**tip** Uncooked kofta and spiced yogurt can be made a day ahead. Cover separately; refrigerate until required.

**per kofta** 3.1g total fat (0.6g saturated fat); 180kJ (43 cal); 0.9g carbohydrate; 3g protein; 0.3g fibre

# sticky pork with kaffir lime leaves

PREPARATION TIME 20 MINUTES  COOKING TIME 20 MINUTES  SERVES 8

You need both the coriander roots and leaves for this recipe.

2 tablespoons peanut oil
300g pork mince
¾ cup (195g) grated palm sugar
⅓ cup (80ml) fish sauce
4 kaffir lime leaves, shredded thinly
½ cup (40g) deep-fried shallots
½ cup (50g) deep-fried garlic
½ cup (70g) coarsely chopped roasted peanuts
1 ½ cups lightly packed fresh coriander leaves
4 kaffir lime leaves, shredded thinly, extra
1 fresh long red chilli, sliced thinly
600g spinach, trimmed
1 lime (60g), cut into wedges

## CORIANDER PASTE
4 coriander roots
5 cloves garlic, chopped
12 white peppercorns

1 Heat half of the oil in large frying pan, add pork; cook, stirring, about 5 minutes or until browned lightly. Drain on absorbent paper; cool.
2 Meanwhile, make coriander paste.
3 Heat remaining oil in large frying pan, cook paste about 1 minute or until fragrant. Add sugar, sauce and lime leaves; simmer, uncovered, about 7 minutes or until thick.
4 Return pork to pan with half the shallots, half the garlic and half the peanuts; cook, uncovered, about 5 minutes or until mixture is sticky.
5 Add remaining shallots, garlic and peanuts. Stir in 1 cup of the coriander leaves and extra lime leaves.
6 Top pork mixture with the remaining coriander and chilli; serve with spinach and lime wedges.

**coriander paste** Wash coriander roots thoroughly; chop coarsely. Using a mortar and pestle or food mill, crush the coriander roots, garlic and peppercorns to form a smooth paste.

**tips** This recipe is best made close to serving.

You can spoon the pork mixture onto the spinach leaves individually on a platter or, if guests are seated, they can assemble their own – it's much quicker.

**per serving** 12.3g total fat (2.5g saturated fat); 1078kJ (258 cal); 26.1g carbohydrate; 12g protein; 2.8g fibre

"This is very simple, but with the fresh, yet complex flavours of kaffir lime and coriander, you'll feel you're eating at a Thai restaurant."

Alexandra Elliott (nee McCowan) worked in the Test Kitchen for 11 years before leaving to become the WW's food editor, and a key member of the 2001 World Food Media Awards, and the 2003 Vittoria Food Media Awards winning team. She has special qualifications in coffee, olive oil tasting and cheese judging.

# mains

A main course is the natural heart of every meal

# lamb cutlets with plum marinade

**PREPARATION TIME** 10 MINUTES (PLUS REFRIGERATION TIME)  **COOKING TIME** 15 MINUTES
SERVES 4

12 lamb cutlets (900g)

PLUM MARINADE
2 tablespoons white vinegar
½ teaspoon ground nutmeg
2 cloves garlic, crushed
2 tablespoons brown sugar
¼ cup (80g) plum jam
⅓ cup (80ml) tomato sauce
1 tablespoon soy sauce
1 tablespoon hot chilli sauce

1 Combine ingredients for plum marinade in large shallow dish; add lamb, turn
to coat in marinade. Cover, refrigerate 3 hours or overnight.
2 Cook lamb on heated oiled grill ( or grill plate or barbecue) until browned and
cooked as desired.
**tip**  Plum marinade is suitable for any cut of lamb.
**per serving**  19.4g total fat (8.9g saturated fat); 1534kJ (367 cal); 25.8g carbohydrate;
23.4g protein; 1.1g fibre

"A spicy, zesty
marinade; I love
using it to jazz up
a lamb roast or
chops cooked on
the barbecue. It's
a hit every time."

Voula Mantzouridis
was a home economist in
the Test Kitchen from 1988
to 1990, leaving to work as a
freelance food consultant and
concentrate on her role as
mother to four children.

# cantonese-style fillet steak

PREPARATION TIME 15 MINUTES (PLUS REFRIGERATION TIME)  COOKING TIME 15 MINUTES
SERVES 4

750g piece beef fillet
2 teaspoons white sugar
2 teaspoons cornflour
1 tablespoon soy sauce
1 tablespoon oyster sauce
2 tablespoons dry sherry
2 medium brown onions (300g)
1½ tablespoons peanut oil
2 cups bean sprouts (160g)

1 Trim all fat and sinew from beef. Cut beef into 5mm-thick slices, flatten slightly with meat mallet. Blend sugar, cornflour and sauces with half of the sherry in medium bowl; add beef, turn to coat in marinade. Cover; refrigerate 3 hours or overnight.

2 Cut onions into thin wedges. Heat 2 teaspoons of the oil in wok; stir-fry onion until just tender, remove from wok.

3 Heat remaining oil in wok; stir-fry beef, in batches, until browned. Return beef to wok with remaining sherry, onion and sprouts; stir-fry until combined.

**per serving** 18.1g total fat (5.9g saturated fat); 1580kJ (378 cal); 9.3g carbohydrate; 42.5g protein; 2.2g fibre

"This was in my first cookbook (*Chinese Cooking Class*), given to me when I was 10 by my mother ... it started my love affair with Chinese cooking."

Cathie Lonnie worked as a chef in northeast Victoria before becoming a food technologist. Three years ago, she moved to Sydney as a home economist in the Test Kitchen; she is now Test Kitchen manager.

# garlic and rosemary smoked lamb

PREPARATION TIME 10 MINUTES (PLUS REFRIGERATION AND SOAKING TIME)

COOKING TIME 50 MINUTES  SERVES 6

1kg boned, rolled lamb loin
4 cloves garlic, halved
8 fresh rosemary sprigs
1 teaspoon dried chilli flakes
1 tablespoon olive oil
250g smoking chips

1  Pierce lamb in eight places with sharp knife; push garlic and rosemary into cuts. Sprinkle lamb with chilli; rub with oil. Cover; refrigerate 3 hours or overnight.

2  Soak smoking chips in large bowl of water 2 hours.

3  Cook lamb, uncovered, on heated oiled barbecue until browned all over. Place drained smoking chips in smoke box on barbecue next to lamb. Cook lamb in covered barbecue, using indirect heat and following manufacturer's instructions, about 40 minutes or until cooked as desired.

tips  Smoking chips and smoke box are available from barbecue specialty shops. When using indirect heat with a gas burner, place the food in a preheated, covered barbecue, then turn the burners directly under the food off, while keeping the side burners on. With a charcoal barbecue, metal bars hold two layers of coals against the sides of the barbecue, leaving the centre of the barbecue rack empty. A disposable aluminium baking dish can be placed here to catch fat drips, if desired.

per serving  17.8g total fat (7.1g saturated fat); 1250kJ (299 cal); 0.2g carbohydrate; 35g protein; 0.3g fibre

"The combination of the rosemary and garlic with smoking chips give this lamb a beautiful flavour and velvety texture."

Sarah O'Brien
was a home economist/stylist in the Test Kitchen from 1999 to 2001. Moving on, she freelanced as a food stylist in Sydney for two years, then left for London and Scotland. Today, she is back here in Australia with her husband and son.

# slow-roasted lamb shanks with caramelised onion and bean puree

PREPARATION TIME 20 MINUTES  COOKING TIME 4 HOURS 30 MINUTES  SERVES 4

1 tablespoon olive oil

8 french-trimmed lamb shanks (2kg)

1 tablespoon white sugar

1½ cups (375ml) dry red wine

2 cups (500ml) beef stock

3 cloves garlic, crushed

20g butter

1 small brown onion (80g), chopped finely

1 trimmed celery stalk (100g), chopped finely

1 tablespoon plain flour

1 tablespoon tomato paste

1 tablespoon coarsely chopped fresh rosemary

## BEAN PUREE

2 x 400g cans cannellini beans, rinsed, drained

1 cup (250ml) chicken stock

4 cloves garlic, crushed

1 tablespoon lemon juice

2 tablespoons olive oil

## CARAMELISED ONION

40g butter

2 medium red onions (340g), sliced thinly

¼ cup (55g) brown sugar

¼ cup (60ml) raspberry vinegar

1 Preheat oven to slow (150°C/130°C fan-forced).

2 Heat oil in large flameproof dish; cook lamb until browned all over. Stir in sugar, wine, stock and garlic; bring to a boil. Transfer lamb to oven; roast, covered, about 4 hours, turning twice during cooking.

3 Meanwhile, make white bean puree and caramelised onion.

4 Remove lamb from dish; cover to keep warm. Pour pan liquids into large heatproof jug. Return dish to heat, melt butter; cook onion and celery, stirring, until celery is just tender. Stir in flour; cook, stirring, 2 minutes. Add reserved pan liquids, paste and rosemary; bring to a boil. Simmer, uncovered, stirring, about 10 minutes or until mixture boils and thickens; strain wine sauce into large heatproof jug.

5 Serve lamb with wine sauce, bean puree and caramelised onion.

bean puree  Combine beans and stock in medium saucepan, bring to a boil; simmer, covered, 20 minutes. Uncover; simmer, stirring occasionally, about 10 minutes or until liquid is absorbed. Blend or process beans, garlic and juice until almost smooth; with motor operating, gradually add oil until mixture is smooth.

caramelised onion  Melt butter in medium saucepan; cook onion, stirring, about 15 minutes or until browned and soft. Stir in sugar and vinegar; cook, stirring, about 15 minutes or until onion is caramelised.

per serving  42.7g total fat (17.5g saturated fat); 3829kJ (916 cal); 46.6g carbohydrate; 70.9g protein; 11.2g fibre

"This is a great winter warmer... and because it goes into the oven for more than four hours, you can relax and forget about it."

Emma Braz
started as a part-time Test Kitchen junior in 1995, and by 2001 was responsible for overseeing the day-to-day operations. Today, she has a business selling gluten-free foods.

"Good company and a glass of wine are all you need with this dish on a cold winter's night."

Margaret lentile
worked in the Test Kitchen from 2001 to 2003, and was the chef for our in-house Test Kitchen catering. She has worked for respected cookery writer Maureen Simpson, and is now with a catering company.

"It's a very simple meat dish, using a humble pork neck; it roasts beautifully, and the flavours of garlic and rosemary are delicious with the pork."

Caroline Jones
was part of the Test Kitchen team from 1993 to 1994. Though Melbourne, her home town, lured her back, she still works in the food industry, as a freelance food consultant, food editor and stylist.

# roast pork with garlic and rosemary

**PREPARATION TIME** 20 MINUTES  **COOKING TIME** 1 HOUR 30 MINUTES  **SERVES** 6

1.5kg pork neck
3 cloves garlic, crushed
1 tablespoon chopped fresh rosemary
1 tablespoon coarse cooking salt
2 tablespoons olive oil
3 bay leaves
1 cup (250ml) water
⅓ cup (80ml) red wine vinegar

1 Preheat oven to moderately hot (200°C/180°C fan-forced).
2 Tie pork with kitchen string at 3cm intervals.
3 Combine garlic, rosemary, salt and oil in small bowl; rub mixture over pork.
4 Place pork on rack in baking dish; add bay leaves, the water and vinegar to dish.
5 Roast pork about 1½ hours or until cooked. Cover pork; stand 10 minutes before slicing.
   **per serving** 26.1g total fat (7.6g saturated fat); 1877kJ (449 cal); 0.2g carbohydrate; 53.1g protein; 0.3g fibre

"With its easy, simple ingredients, it's a very different meatloaf – it's moist, feeds lots of people, it's not expensive and it's DAMN good."

Sarah Coryton (nee Dewhurst) worked in the Test Kitchen from 1968 until 1971 as then food editor Ellen Sinclair's personal assistant. She became a "good buddy" of present food director Pamela Clark and they have kept up the happy connection since.

# savoury-glazed meatloaf

**PREPARATION TIME** 15 MINUTES  **COOKING TIME** 1 HOUR 15 MINUTES  **SERVES** 4

750g beef mince

1 cup (70g) stale breadcrumbs

1 medium brown onion (150g), chopped finely

1 egg

1 tablespoon worcestershire sauce

2 tablespoons tomato sauce

185g can evaporated milk

2 teaspoons mustard powder

1 tablespoon brown sugar

½ teaspoon mustard powder, extra

¼ cup (60ml) tomato sauce, extra

1 Preheat oven to moderate (180°C/160°C fan-forced). Grease 14cm x 21cm loaf pan.

2 Combine beef, breadcrumbs, onion, egg, sauces, milk and mustard in medium bowl; press mixture into pan. Turn pan upside down onto a foil-lined oven tray. Leave pan in place. Cook 15 minutes.

3 Meanwhile, combine sugar, extra mustard and extra sauce in small bowl.

4 Remove loaf from oven; remove pan. Brush loaf well with glaze, return loaf to oven; cook 1 hour or until well browned and cooked through. Serve with rocket leaves and balsamic dressing, if desired.

**per serving**  19.9g total fat (10g saturated fat); 1986kJ (475 cal); 29.1g carbohydrate; 45.8g protein; 1.8g fibre

# rogan josh

PREPARATION TIME 15 MINUTES (PLUS REFRIGERATION TIME)
COOKING TIME 2 HOURS  SERVES 4

A Kashmiri speciality using only the most tender young lamb available from this mountainous province in north India.

1kg diced lamb
1 cup (280g) yogurt
1 tablespoon malt vinegar
4 cloves garlic, crushed
4cm piece fresh ginger (20g), grated
2 tablespoons ghee
4 cardamom pods, bruised
3 cloves
1 cinnamon stick
2 medium brown onions (300g), chopped finely
3 teaspoons ground cumin
1 tablespoon ground coriander
1 teaspoon ground fennel
1½ teaspoons sweet paprika
¾ teaspoon chilli powder
1¼ cups (310ml) chicken stock
1 teaspoon garam masala
2 tablespoons finely chopped fresh coriander
1 tablespoon finely chopped fresh mint

1 Combine lamb, yogurt, vinegar, half the garlic and half the ginger in large bowl; mix well. Cover; refrigerate 3 hours or overnight.

2 Heat ghee in large frying pan, add cardamom, cloves and cinnamon; cook, stirring, until fragrant.

3 Add onion, remaining garlic and remaining ginger; cook, stirring, until onion is browned lightly.

4 Add cumin, ground coriander, fennel, paprika and chilli; cook, stirring, until fragrant. Add lamb mixture; stir to coat in spice mixture.

5 Add stock, bring to a boil; reduce heat, simmer, covered, 1½ hours. Uncover; simmer further 15 minutes or until lamb is tender. Just before serving, stir in garam masala. Sprinkle with fresh herbs and serve with basmati rice, if desired.

**tip**  Recipe can be made a day ahead; keep, covered, in refrigerator.

**per serving**  33.4g total fat (17.4g saturated fat); 2349kJ (562 cal); 8g carbohydrate; 57.3g protein; 1.2g fibre

"This is winter comfort food for me. I like to make it on a weekend to eat through the week."

Sophia Young
was a New York-trained chef before she began in the Test Kitchen in 1993. She became an in-house food stylist, but was lured away to *Australian Gourmet Traveller* as associate food editor, staying there until early 2005. Sophia is now the food editor of a food and lifestyle magazine.

"I have tried several osso buco recipes and always come back to this. It is such a flavoursome one-pot wonder."
Jane Hann
has worked on the WW cookbooks as a freelance food stylist since 1991, and been part of the evolving look of the pages. Based in Sydney, she juggles food styling with raising three sons.

# osso buco

PREPARATION TIME 30 MINUTES  COOKING TIME 2 HOURS  SERVES 6

The name means "hollow bones". Osso buco is served throughout Italy, but is a specialty of Milan.

90g butter
2 medium carrots (240g), chopped finely
2 large brown onions (400g), chopped finely
3 trimmed celery stalks (300g), chopped finely
2 cloves garlic, crushed
2kg veal shin or osso buco
⅓ cup (50g) plain flour, approximately, for dusting
2 tablespoons olive oil
2 x 400g cans chopped tomatoes
½ cup (125ml) dry red wine
1¾ cups (430ml) beef stock
1 tablespoon finely chopped fresh basil
1 teaspoon finely chopped fresh thyme
1 bay leaf
2.5cm strip lemon rind
¼ cup finely chopped fresh flat-leaf parsley
1 teaspoon grated lemon rind

1 Heat a third of the butter in large saucepan; cook carrot, onion, celery and half of the garlic until onion is golden brown. Remove from heat; transfer vegetables to large ovenproof dish.

2 Coat veal with flour; shake away excess. Heat remaining butter and oil in same pan. Add veal; brown well on all sides. Carefully pack veal on top of vegetables.

3 Preheat oven to moderate (180°C/160°C fan-forced).

4 Drain fat from pan. Add undrained tomatoes, wine, stock, basil, thyme, bay leaf and strip of lemon rind; bring sauce to a boil.

5 Pour sauce over veal. Cover dish; bake in oven about 1½ hours, stirring occasionally, or until veal is very tender. Serve, sprinkled with combined remaining garlic, parsley and grated lemon rind.

**per serving**  22.3g total fat (10g saturated fat); 2103kJ (503 cal); 17.5g carbohydrate; 54.3g protein; 5g fibre

# port and balsamic slow-roasted lamb

**PREPARATION TIME** 15 MINUTES  **COOKING TIME** 6 HOURS 55 MINUTES  **SERVES** 6

2.5kg leg of lamb
¼ cup (30g) sea salt flakes
20g butter
1 tablespoon olive oil
⅓ cup (80ml) dry red wine
⅓ cup (80ml) balsamic vinegar
⅓ cup (80ml) port
¼ cup (60ml) beef stock
8 cloves garlic, crushed
8 medium egg tomatoes (600g), halved lengthways

1 Preheat oven to very slow (120°C/100°C fan-forced).
2 Bring a large saucepan of water to a boil; add lamb, simmer 15 minutes. Drain; pat lamb dry. Pierce lamb all over with sharp knife; press salt into cuts.
3 Heat butter and oil in large flameproof dish; cook lamb, turning, until browned all over. Add wine, vinegar, port, stock and garlic to dish. Roast lamb, in oven, covered, 4½ hours.
4 Add tomatoes, cut-side up; roast further 2 hours, uncovered, basting occasionally.
5 Remove lamb and tomatoes from dish. Boil pan juices until reduced by half; serve with lamb.

**per serving**  22.7g total fat (9.7g saturated fat); 2186kJ (52 cal); 4.5g carbohydrate; 69.6g protein; 2.1g fibre

"This recipe introduced me to slow-roast cooking. It's a winter standard in our house."

Nadia French came to the Test Kitchen in 1996 as "the shopping girl". By the time she left – to have the first of three babies – she was cooking for photography. Today, she has a business with Emma Braz (page 51).

# nam jim chicken

PREPARATION TIME 20 MINUTES  COOKING TIME 20 MINUTES  SERVES 4

8 chicken thigh fillets (880g)

1 teaspoon ground cumin

1 teaspoon ground coriander

2 tablespoons grated palm sugar

1 cup loosely packed fresh thai basil leaves

1 cup loosely packed fresh coriander leaves

3 cups (240g) bean sprouts

3 long green chillies, chopped coarsely

2 cloves garlic, quartered

10cm stick (20g) fresh lemon grass, sliced thinly

3 green onions, chopped coarsely

1 coriander root, chopped coarsely

¼ cup (60ml) lime juice

1 tablespoon fish sauce

2 tablespoons grated palm sugar, extra

1 Combine chicken in large bowl with ground spices and sugar. Cook chicken in large oiled frying pan until cooked through. Serve on combined herbs and sprouts.

2 Meanwhile, blend or process remaining ingredients until smooth; spoon over chicken.

**per serving**  16g total fat (4.9g saturated fat); 1580kJ (378 cal); 14.9g carbohydrate; 44g protein; 2.9g fibre

"Very yummy, super easy and the nicest low-fat dish I ever developed. Easy sauce to use with fish, too."

Sammie Coryton daughter of Sarah Coryton (page 53), was a home economist in the Test Kitchen before being poached to work in TV, as supervising chef on *Fresh with The Australian Women's Weekly*, on the Nine Network.

# lamb and apricot tagine with citrus couscous

PREPARATION TIME 20 MINUTES (PLUS STANDING TIME)  COOKING TIME 1 HOUR 10 MINUTES
SERVES 8

1⅔ cups (250g) dried apricots
¾ cup (180ml) orange juice
½ cup (125ml) boiling water
2 tablespoons olive oil
900g lamb steaks, chopped coarsely
2 medium red capsicums (400g), chopped coarsely
1 large brown onion (200g), chopped coarsely
2 medium kumara (800g), chopped coarsely
3 cloves garlic, crushed
1 teaspoon ground cinnamon
2 teaspoons ground cumin
2 teaspoons ground coriander
1 cup (250ml) dry red wine
1 litre (4 cups) chicken stock
2 tablespoons honey
1 cup loosely packed fresh coriander leaves
¾ cup (200g) low-fat yogurt

### CITRUS COUSCOUS
1 litre (4 cups) water
4 cups (800g) couscous
1 tablespoon finely grated orange rind
2 teaspoons finely grated lemon rind
2 teaspoons finely grated lime rind

1 Combine apricots, juice and the water in small heatproof bowl. Cover; stand 45 minutes.
2 Meanwhile, heat half of the oil in large saucepan; cook lamb, in batches, until browned all over.
3 Heat remaining oil in same pan; cook capsicum, onion, kumara, garlic and ground spices, stirring, until onion softens and mixture is fragrant. Add wine; bring to a boil. Reduce heat; simmer, uncovered, about 5 minutes or until liquid reduces by half.
4 Return lamb to pan with undrained apricots, stock and honey; bring to a boil. Reduce heat; simmer, covered, about 50 minutes or until lamb is tender. Remove from heat; stir in fresh coriander.
5 Meanwhile, make citrus couscous.
6 Serve lamb and apricot tagine on citrus couscous; drizzle with yogurt.
   citrus couscous  Bring the water to a boil in medium saucepan; stir in couscous and rinds. Remove from heat; stand, covered, about 5 minutes or until liquid is absorbed, fluffing with fork occasionally to separate grains.
   per serving  15.9g total fat (5.5g saturated fat); 3369kJ (806 cal); 115.9g carbohydrate; 43.6g protein; 6.6g fibre

"This hearty dish has so many of the flavours I love... spicy, fragrant, savoury and sweet."

Helen Webster worked as a home economist in the UK food industry before immigrating to Australia and coming to work in the Test Kitchen. Today, she is a freelance food stylist.

# satay beef and stir-fried vegetables with rice

PREPARATION TIME 20 MINUTES  COOKING TIME 20 MINUTES  SERVES 4

1 litre (4 cups) water
1 cup (200g) basmati rice
1 teaspoon peanut oil
500g lean beef topside, sliced thinly
1 large brown onion (200g), sliced thinly
1 clove garlic, crushed
2cm piece fresh ginger (10g), grated
2 fresh small red thai chillies, chopped finely
1 medium red capsicum (200g), chopped coarsely
1 medium green capsicum (200g), chopped coarsely
100g mushrooms, halved
225g can bamboo shoots, drained
1 teaspoon curry powder
2 teaspoons cornflour
½ cup (125ml) chicken stock
¼ cup (70g) light smooth peanut butter
2 tablespoons oyster sauce
1 tablespoon unsalted, roasted, coarsely chopped peanuts

1 Bring the water to a boil in large saucepan; stir in rice. Boil, uncovered, about 15 minutes or until rice is just tender. Drain, rinse under hot water; drain rice again, cover to keep warm.

2 Meanwhile, heat oil in wok; stir-fry beef, in batches, until browned all over.

3 Add onion and garlic to wok; stir-fry until onion softens. Add ginger, chilli, capsicums, mushrooms, bamboo shoots and curry powder; stir-fry until vegetables are just tender.

4 Blend cornflour with stock in small jug, pour into wok; stir to combine with vegetable mixture. Return beef to wok with peanut butter and sauce; bring to a boil, stirring, until sauce thickens slightly and beef is cooked as desired. Stir in peanuts; serve with rice.

tip You can use sliced lamb fillets or sliced chicken thigh fillets instead of the beef, if you prefer.

per serving 19.4g total fat (5.1g saturated fat); 2249kJ (538 cal); 51.4g carbohydrate; 39.1g protein; 5.6g fibre

"I'm always on the lookout for great-tasting recipes that aren't expensive and please everyone, and this fits the bill."

Joan Chippindale was at St George County Council in Sydney, from 1963 to 1967, first as a junior, then becoming senior cooking teacher/demonstrator. She worked in the Test Kitchen in the early '70s. Joan later worked for a stove manufacturer.

# thelma's baked kibbeh

**PREPARATION TIME** 1 HOUR **COOKING TIME** 1 HOUR 40 MINUTES **SERVES** 8

1½ cups (240g) burghul
2 teaspoons coarse cooking salt
1 large brown onion (200g), chopped finely
500g finely minced lamb
1 teaspoon ground black pepper
1 teaspoon ground allspice
½ cup (125ml) iced water
20g butter
½ cup (125ml) olive oil

## FILLING

2 teaspoons olive oil
250g coarsely minced lamb
1 medium brown onion (150g), chopped finely
1 teaspoon ground allspice
½ teaspoon ground cinnamon
½ teaspoon ground nutmeg
1 teaspoon coarse cooking salt
½ teaspoon ground white pepper
¾ cup (120g) pine nuts, toasted

1 Oil 25cm x 32cm baking dish.
2 Cover burghul with cold water in medium bowl; stand 10 minutes.
3 Meanwhile, sprinkle salt over onion; stand 10 minutes.
4 Make filling.
5 Drain burghul, squeezing with hands to remove as much water as possible.
6 Rinse onion under cold water; squeeze dry in absorbent paper.
7 Combine burghul, onion, lamb, pepper, allspice and the iced water in large bowl; knead about 10 minutes or until mixture forms a smooth paste. (To ensure kibbeh mixture stays cold and smooth, knead in a small piece of ice from time to time.)
8 Using wet hands, press half the kibbeh mixture evenly over base of dish.
9 Preheat oven to moderate (180°C/160°C fan-forced).
10 Drain away oil from filling; spread filling evenly over kibbeh layer. Shape remaining kibbeh mixture into large patties; place patties over filling. Using wet hands, join patties to cover filling completely; smooth top with wet hands. Using wet knife, cut through kibbeh to form diamond shapes. Dot each diamond with a pinch of butter.
11 Drizzle kibbeh evenly with oil. Cook, uncovered, about 1½ hours or until kibbeh is cooked through. Drain away excess oil before serving.

**filling** Heat oil in medium frying pan; cook lamb, stirring, over high heat, until browned all over. Add onion; cook, stirring, until browned lightly. Stir in spices and seasonings; remove from heat, stir in nuts.

per serving 34.8g total fat (7.1g saturated fat); 2061kJ (493 cal); 20.9g carbohydrate; 24.9g protein; 6.2g fibre

"My mother-in-law's recipe had never been written down – she cooks by feel and instinct – until I badgered her into making it with me."

Karen Hammial
was the founding editor of *Australian Gourmet Traveller*, working on it for a decade before trying marketing and publishing. She returned to food and cooking, and has been food editor of the WW cookbooks for seven years.

"My favourite quick
Asian meal for
something different
at dinner time."

Sophia North
(nee Dickson) worked in
the Test Kitchen on *Cooking
Class Japanese* and many
others. She has now married,
runs a catering business
with her husband, works as
a private chef and, in 2003,
became a mum!

# sweet soy beef on rice

PREPARATION TIME 10 MINUTES  COOKING TIME 15 MINUTES  SERVES 4

Shirataki translates from Japanese as white waterfall, which rather romantically
describes these transparent thin noodles that are sold fresh in water packs.

2 cups (400g) koshihikari rice
200g shirataki, drained
½ cup (125ml) japanese soy sauce
1 tablespoon white sugar
¼ cup (60ml) mirin or sweet white wine
300g beef eye fillet, sliced paper thin
2 green onions, sliced diagonally into 2cm lengths
1cm piece fresh ginger (5g), grated finely

1 Cook rice in large saucepan of boiling water until just tender; drain, cover
  to keep warm.
2 Meanwhile, place noodles in medium saucepan of boiling water. Cook
  1 minute, separating noodles. Drain noodles, cut into 10cm lengths.
3 Bring sauce, sugar and mirin to a boil in medium saucepan. Add beef;
  cook, stirring, until beef just changes colour. Strain beef over medium
  heatproof bowl; return sauce to same pan.
4 Add onion and noodles to pan, simmer about 3 minutes or until onion
  softens. Return beef to pan, add ginger, stir until heated through.
5 Divide rice among serving bowls. Top with beef mixture.
  **tips** You can substitute rice or cellophane noodles for the shirataki noodles.
  Beef will be easier to slice finely if it's been placed in the freezer for about
  an hour before cutting.
  **per serving**  4.9g total fat (2g saturated fat); 2282kJ (546 cal); 97.5g carbohydrate;
  24.4g protein; 7.8g fibre

"Great as an entertaining dish, or perfect for a Sunday night family gathering. The tanginess of the lemon gives potatoes another dimension."

Bronwen Warden (nee Clark) has a degree in Applied Science – Food and Nutrition. She worked in the Test Kitchen for two years before going overseas. Returning, she became assistant food editor for *Australian Gourmet Traveller* for six years, and now works with Neil Perry designing menus for Qantas.

# roast garlic lamb with lemon potatoes

**PREPARATION TIME** 25 MINUTES (PLUS REFRIGERATION TIME)  **COOKING TIME** 1 HOUR 40 MINUTES
SERVES 6

½ cup (125ml) olive oil
2 tablespoons finely grated lemon rind
2 tablespoons lemon juice
2 tablespoons dry white wine
1 teaspoon cracked black peppercorns
2 tablespoons finely chopped fresh thyme
2kg leg of lamb
2 cloves garlic, sliced
1 tablespoon fresh rosemary leaves

### LEMON POTATOES
2kg potatoes
¼ cup (60ml) olive oil
1 tablespoon finely grated lemon rind
⅓ cup (80ml) lemon juice
2 tablespoons finely chopped fresh rosemary
2 tablespoons finely chopped fresh thyme
1 teaspoon cracked black peppercorns

1 Combine oil, rind, juice, wine, pepper and thyme in medium jug; mix well.
2 Using point of knife, make 12 cuts evenly over top of lamb leg. Place a slice of garlic and some of the rosemary leaves in each cut. Place lamb in large bowl.
3 Pour oil mixture over lamb; cover, refrigerate, turning lamb occasionally, for 3 hours or overnight.
4 Preheat oven to moderately hot (200°C/180°C fan-forced).
5 Drain lamb over bowl; reserve marinade. Place lamb in large baking dish, roast, uncovered, 40 minutes. Meanwhile, prepare lemon potatoes. Place potatoes in oven with lamb; roast further 50 minutes, turning potatoes occasionally, or until lamb and potatoes are tender.
6 Remove lamb from dish; cover to keep warm. Drain juices from dish; reserve juices.
7 Heat reserved marinade and reserved juices in small saucepan, bring to a boil; serve with sliced lamb and lemon potatoes.
**lemon potatoes** Cut potatoes into 3cm pieces, place in large baking dish. Pour over combined remaining ingredients; mix well.
**per serving** 43.4g total fat (11.2g saturated fat); 3344kJ (800 cal); 38.2g carbohydrate; 61.8g protein; 4.9g fibre

# lamb shank stew with creamy mash

**PREPARATION TIME** 20 MINUTES  **COOKING TIME** 3 HOURS 20 MINUTES  **SERVES** 8

8 french-trimmed lamb shanks (2kg)
8 cloves garlic, halved
2 medium lemons (280g)
2 tablespoons olive oil
3 large brown onions (600g), chopped coarsely
2 cups (500ml) dry red wine
3 medium carrots (360g), quartered lengthways
3 trimmed celery stalks (300g), chopped coarsely
4 bay leaves
8 sprigs fresh thyme
1.75 litres (7 cups) chicken stock
½ cup finely chopped fresh flat-leaf parsley
¼ cup finely chopped fresh mint
2kg potatoes, chopped coarsely
300ml cream, warmed
100g butter

1  Pierce the meatiest part of each shank in two places with sharp knife; press garlic into cuts.
2  Grate rind of both lemons finely; reserve. Halve lemons; rub cut sides all over shanks.
3  Preheat oven to moderate (180°C/160°C fan-forced).
4  Heat oil in large flameproof casserole dish; cook shanks, in batches, until browned. Cook onion, stirring, in same dish until softened. Add wine; bring to a boil; remove dish from heat.
5  Place carrot, celery and shanks, in alternate layers, on onion mixture in dish. Top with bay leaves and thyme; carefully pour stock over the top. Cover dish tightly with lid or foil; cook in oven about 3 hours or until meat is tender.
6  Meanwhile, combine grated rind, parsley and mint in small bowl.
7  Boil, steam or microwave potato until tender; drain. Mash potato with warmed cream and butter in large bowl until smooth. Cover to keep warm.
8  Transfer shanks to platter; cover to keep warm. Strain pan juices through muslin-lined sieve or colander into medium saucepan; discard solids. Boil pan juices, uncovered, stirring occasionally, until reduced by half.
9  Divide mashed potato among serving plates; top with shanks, sprinkle with lemon-herb mixture, drizzle with pan juices. Serve with steamed green beans, if desired.

**per serving** 40.2g total fat (22.2g saturated fat); 3001kJ (718 cal); 38.6g carbohydrate; 39.3g protein; 7.9g fibre

"I just love lamb shanks, and find them very therapeutic to cook, especially on a wintry afternoon."

Kate Tait
is a chef who joined the Test Kitchen to develop material for the WW cookbooks, and *Woman's Day* and WW magazines. She became assistant food editor *of Australian Gourmet Traveller*, leaving to pursue a freelance career as a home economist.

# chicken parmesan with basil sauce

PREPARATION TIME 25 MINUTES   COOKING TIME 35 MINUTES   SERVES 4

1 cup (70g) stale breadcrumbs
⅓ cup (25g) coarsely grated parmesan
1 tablespoon finely chopped fresh flat-leaf parsley
3 bacon rashers (210g), chopped finely
80g butter, melted
2 cloves garlic, crushed
1 teaspoon worcestershire sauce
½ teaspoon mustard powder
4 single chicken breast fillets (800g)

BASIL SAUCE
⅓ cup (80ml) olive oil
¼ cup (60ml) white vinegar
1 clove garlic
1 cup firmly packed fresh basil leaves
⅓ cup (80ml) cream
1 egg yolk

1 Preheat oven to moderate (180°C/160°C fan-forced).
2 Combine breadcrumbs, cheese and parsley in large bowl.
3 Cook bacon in large non-stick frying pan until crisp; drain on absorbent paper. Add bacon to breadcrumb mixture.
4 Combine butter, garlic, sauce and mustard in shallow dish.
5 Dip chicken into butter mixture; place chicken, in single layer, in shallow ovenproof dish. Press crumb mixture on top of chicken.
6 Cook, uncovered, about 25 minutes or until chicken is cooked through.
7 Meanwhile, make basil sauce.
8 Serve chicken with basil sauce, and a green salad, if desired.
   **basil sauce**  Blend oil, vinegar, garlic, basil and cream until smooth. Pour sauce into small saucepan, add egg yolk; whisk over low heat, without boiling, until sauce thickens slightly.
   **per serving**  54.5g total fat (23.1g saturated fat); 3210kJ (768 cal); 12.9g carbohydrate; 57.2g protein; 1.4g fibre

"An uncomplicated recipe that can be prepared as an everyday meal, or a 'glam' one for special occasions."

Kerry Park
joined the Test Kitchen in 1971 after working and studying in the UK and Europe. She then married and moved with her husband to Papua New Guinea. She now has two children and lives in Brisbane.

# curried chicken pies

PREPARATION TIME 50 MINUTES  COOKING TIME 1 HOUR 45 MINUTES (PLUS STANDING TIME)
SERVES 6

1.6kg chicken
90g butter
1 small leek (200g), chopped finely
1 medium white onion (150g), chopped finely
1 medium red capsicum (200g), chopped finely
2 trimmed celery stalks (200g), chopped finely
3 teaspoons curry powder
¼ teaspoon chilli powder
¼ cup (35g) plain flour
⅓ cup (80g) sour cream
½ cup finely chopped fresh flat-leaf parsley
2 sheets ready-rolled puff pastry
1 egg, beaten lightly

1 Place chicken in large saucepan, add enough water to just cover chicken;
   bring to a boil, reduce heat, simmer, uncovered, 1 hour. Remove from heat;
   when cool enough to handle, remove from stock. Reserve 1¾ cups (430ml)
   of the stock for this recipe.

2 Preheat oven to moderately hot (200°C/180°C fan-forced).

3 Remove skin and bones from chicken; chop chicken flesh roughly.

4 Heat butter in large frying pan, add leek, onion, capsicum and celery; cook,
   stirring, until vegetables are soft.

5 Add curry powder and chilli powder; cook, stirring, until fragrant. Stir in flour.
   Add reserved stock, stir over heat until mixture boils and thickens; reduce heat,
   simmer 1 minute, remove from heat.

6 Add sour cream, chicken and parsley to vegetable mixture. Spoon mixture into
   six 1¼-cup (310ml) ovenproof dishes.

7 Cut pastry into six rounds large enough to cover top of each dish. Lightly brush
   pastry with egg. Place pies on oven tray.

8 Bake pies 10 minutes; reduce temperature to moderate (180°C/160°C fan-forced),
   bake further 15 minutes or until pastry is golden brown.

   **tip** Filling can be made a day ahead; keep, covered, in refrigerator.

   **per serving** 52.8g total fat (25.4g saturated fat); 3001kJ (718 cal); 28.5g carbohydrate;
   33.3g protein; 3g fibre

"I make individual
pies as they freeze
beautifully and are
great when there's
a large crowd for
dinner, as they
remain hot."

Rosemary Wellington
worked in the Test Kitchen
in the late 1970s. She left to
cook at Crank's Restaurant
in London and test recipes
for their cookbook. She
now makes menswear in
Melbourne – and still cooks.

# twice-cooked chicken with asian greens

**PREPARATION TIME** 45 MINUTES

**COOKING TIME** 1 HOUR 10 MINUTES (PLUS STANDING AND REFRIGERATION TIME)  **SERVES** 4

2.5 litres (10 cups) water
1 litre (4 cups) chicken stock
2 cups (500ml) chinese cooking wine
8 cloves garlic, crushed
10cm piece fresh ginger (50g), sliced thinly
1 teaspoon sesame oil
1.6kg chicken
peanut oil, for deep-frying
1 tablespoon peanut oil, extra
150g snow peas, trimmed
500g choy sum, chopped coarsely
350g chinese broccoli, chopped coarsely
2 green onions, sliced thinly

## CHAR SIU DRESSING
2 cloves garlic, crushed
5cm piece fresh ginger (25g), grated finely
¼ cup (60ml) char siu sauce
2 tablespoons soy sauce
1 teaspoon white sugar
1 tablespoon rice vinegar

1 Combine the water, stock, wine, garlic, ginger and sesame oil in large saucepan; bring to a boil. Boil, uncovered, 10 minutes. Add chicken, reduce heat; simmer, uncovered, 15 minutes. Remove from heat, cover; stand chicken in stock 3 hours. Remove chicken; pat dry with absorbent paper. Reserve stock for another use.

2 Using sharp knife or kitchen scissors, halve chicken lengthways; cut halves crossways through the centre. Cut breasts from wings and thighs from legs to give eight chicken pieces in total. Cut wings in half; cut breast and thighs into thirds. Place chicken pieces on tray; refrigerate, uncovered, 3 hours or overnight.

3 Meanwhile, make char siu dressing.

4 Heat peanut oil for deep-frying in wok; deep-fry chicken, in batches, until browned. Drain on absorbent paper.

5 Heat extra 1 tablespoon of peanut oil in cleaned wok; stir-fry snow peas, choy sum and chinese broccoli until just tender. Add 2 tablespoons of the char siu dressing; stir-fry to combine.

6 Divide vegetables among serving plates; top with chicken, drizzle with remaining dressing, sprinkle with onion.

**char siu dressing** Stir garlic, ginger, sauces and sugar over heat in small saucepan until mixture comes to a boil. Remove from heat; stir in vinegar.

**per serving** 52.9g total fat (14g saturated fat); 3382kJ (809 cal); 18.3g carbohydrate; 43.8g protein; 8.9g fibre

"I love the whole process of making this recipe – and it tastes great."

Kirrily Smith
is currently working in the Test Kitchen, after starting her career as an apprentice pastry chef. She began as a junior and is moving up through the ranks.

# barbecued chicken with sweet chilli vinegar sauce

PREPARATION TIME 20 MINUTES (PLUS REFRIGERATION TIME)
COOKING TIME 20 MINUTES (PLUS COOLING TIME) SERVES 4

1kg chicken thigh fillets
2 tablespoons peanut oil
½ cup (125ml) coconut milk

PASTE
4 cloves garlic, crushed
1 teaspoon cracked black peppercorns
2 teaspoons white sugar
2 teaspoons ground turmeric
2 teaspoons hot paprika
1 tablespoon chopped fresh coriander root
1 teaspoon curry powder
2 fresh small red thai chillies, chopped
1 tablespoon peanut oil

SWEET CHILLI VINEGAR SAUCE
6 fresh small red thai chillies, chopped coarsely
4 cloves garlic, quartered
1 cup (250ml) white vinegar
½ cup (110g) caster sugar
1 teaspoon coarse cooking salt
1 teaspoon tamarind paste

1  Using mortar and pestle, crush ingredients for paste.
2  Cut chicken in half, combine with paste and oil in large bowl; cover, refrigerate
   3 hours or overnight.
3  Cook chicken on barbecue (or grill or grill plate), basting frequently with coconut
   milk, until browned and cooked through.
4  Meanwhile, make sweet chilli vinegar sauce.
5  Serve chicken with sauce, and salad greens, if desired.
   **sweet chilli vinegar sauce**  Place ingredients in small saucepan, stir over heat,
   without boiling, until sugar is dissolved. Bring to a boil, simmer, uncovered, about
   15 minutes or until slightly thickened; cool 5 minutes. Blend or process mixture
   until chopped finely.
   **tips**  Paste can be made a week ahead; keep, covered, in refrigerator. Sauce
   can be made a day ahead; keep, covered, in refrigerator.
   Chicken best cooked just before serving.
   **per serving**  38.3g total fat (13.7g saturated fat); 2759kJ (660 cal); 31.8g carbohydrate;
   47.6g protein; 1.7g fibre

"This is so good cooked on the barbecue that my family never wants takeaway, they want me to cook it for them, instead."
Helen Rowsell studied at Western Sydney University, was a part-time gym instructor, then joined the Test Kitchen in 1993. She moved on to testing kitchen appliances, and now lives in Tamworth, NSW, with her husband and three children.

# basic pizza dough

PREPARATION TIME 20 MINUTES
(PLUS STANDING TIME)

2 teaspoons (7g) dried yeast
½ teaspoon white sugar
¾ cup (180ml) warm water
2 cups (300g) plain flour
1 teaspoon coarse cooking salt
2 tablespoons olive oil

1 Combine yeast, sugar and the water in small bowl; cover, stand in warm place about 10 minutes or until frothy.
2 Sift flour and salt into large bowl, stir in yeast mixture and oil, mix to a soft dough. Turn dough onto floured surface; knead about 5 minutes or until smooth and elastic.
3 Place dough in oiled bowl, cover; stand in warm place about 1 hour or until doubled in size.
4 Knead dough on floured surface until smooth; roll out to fit 30cm pizza tray.
tip Make dough on day of baking.

# basic tomato sauce

PREPARATION TIME 10 MINUTES
COOKING TIME 20 MINUTES

1 tablespoon olive oil
1 small white onion (80g), chopped finely
2 cloves garlic, crushed
400g can chopped tomatoes
¼ cup (70g) tomato paste
1 teaspoon white sugar
1 tablespoon finely chopped fresh oregano
1 tablespoon finely chopped fresh basil

1 Heat oil in medium frying pan, add onion and garlic; cook, stirring, until onion is soft.
2 Add undrained tomatoes, tomato paste, sugar and oregano. Simmer, uncovered, about 15 minutes or until mixture is thick. Stir in basil.
tip Sauce can be made two days ahead; keep, covered in refrigerator.

"I love making pizza at home... and this versatile and easy dough can also be used for loaves, rolls, foccacia – anything."

Cynthia Black
came to the Test Kitchen in the early 1990s, and left in 1993, continuing her food career at Darling Mills, her family's restaurant in Sydney. She has now gone into business for herself, selling olives, dips and sauces.

# prosciutto and bocconcini pizza

PREPARATION TIME 15 MINUTES   COOKING TIME 20 MINUTES   MAKES 8 SLICES

1 quantity basic pizza dough
½ quantity basic tomato sauce
6 slices prosciutto (90g)
100g bocconcini, sliced
12 fresh baby basil leaves

1 Preheat oven to hot (220°C/200°C fan-forced).
2 Roll pizza dough on floured surface to a 30cm round; place on oiled pizza tray or oven tray. Spread with basic tomato sauce.
3 Arrange prosciutto and bocconcini over tomato sauce.
4 Bake about 20 minutes, or until base is well browned and crisp.
5 Serve sprinkled with basil.
per slice 8.8g total fat (2.4g saturated fat); 978kJ (234 cal); 29.3g carbohydrate; 9g protein; 2.3g fibre

# crab in black bean sauce

**PREPARATION TIME** 30 MINUTES (PLUS FREEZING TIME) **COOKING TIME** 25 MINUTES **SERVES** 4

2 uncooked mud crabs (1.5kg)
1½ tablespoons packaged salted black beans
1 tablespoon peanut oil
1 clove garlic, crushed
1cm piece fresh ginger (5g), grated finely
½ teaspoon sambal oelek
1 tablespoon soy sauce
1 teaspoon white sugar
1 tablespoon chinese cooking wine
¾ cup (180ml) chicken stock
2 green onions, sliced diagonally

1 Place crabs in freezer for at least 2 hours. Slide a sharp strong knife under top of shell at back of each crab, lever off shell and discard. Remove and discard gills; wash crabs thoroughly. Chop body into quarters with cleaver. Remove claws and nippers; chop nippers into large pieces.
2 Rinse beans well under cold water, drain; mash beans lightly.
3 Heat oil in wok; stir-fry garlic, ginger and sambal until fragrant. Add beans, sauce, sugar, wine and stock; bring to a boil.
4 Add all of the crab; cook, covered, about 15 minutes or until crab has changed in colour. Place crab on serving plate; pour over sauce, top with onion.
**per serving** 5.9g total fat (1.1g saturated fat); 711kJ (170 cal); 5.2g carbohydrate; 23.6g protein; 0.6g fibre

"The girls in the Test Kitchen called my grandmother 'Mrs S', but to our family she was Momma. And she had two passions in life – her food and her family. This dish was a real favourite of hers."

Amy Sinclair
is the grand-daughter of Ellen Sinclair, who was food editor from 1968 to 1983.

# chinese fish

**PREPARATION TIME** 10 MINUTES  **COOKING TIME** 20 MINUTES  **SERVES** 2

2cm piece fresh ginger (10g), chopped coarsely
2 whole snapper or bream (500g)
¼ cup (60ml) soy sauce
5cm piece fresh ginger (25g), cut into thin strips, extra
6 green onions, sliced thinly
¼ cup (60ml) peanut oil

1 Fill a large frying pan two-thirds full with water. Add chopped ginger; bring to a boil, boil 5 minutes. Reduce heat, carefully add fish to water; simmer, covered, about 10 minutes or until fish is just cooked through.
2 Remove fish from water. Drain on absorbent paper, place on serving plates.
3 Pour sauce over fish, sprinkle with extra ginger and onion. Heat oil in small saucepan until very hot; pour hot oil over fish.

**tips** This dish is a popular item on Chinese menus. It is light and full of flavour. Serve the fish by itself, or with boiled rice as an accompaniment.
The recipe serves two, or four if part of a Chinese meal where there are other dishes being served.

**per serving** 29g total fat (5.5g saturated fat); 1496kJ (358 cal); 3.1g carbohydrate; 21.6g protein; 1.2g fibre

"When I developed this, I remember Ellen Sinclair saying how easy it was to cook the fish and get a great result."

Penny Yan
started in advertising, but moved to the Test Kitchen and "fell in love with the job". She helped develop many classic Test Kitchen recipes. Penny is now retired.

# octopus in red wine

**PREPARATION TIME** 25 MINUTES **COOKING TIME** 1 HOUR AND 45 MINUTES **SERVES** 4

1 tablespoon olive oil

2kg whole cleaned baby octopus, quartered

2 cloves garlic, crushed

500g baby brown onions, quartered

2 bay leaves

1½ cups (375ml) dry red wine

1 cup (250ml) chicken stock

¼ cup (60ml) red wine vinegar

440ml can tomato puree

2 teaspoons dried oregano

2 teaspoons white sugar

1 tablespoon finely chopped fresh flat-leaf parsley

**1** Heat oil in large saucepan, cook octopus and garlic, stirring, until almost dry.

**2** Add onion, bay leaves, wine, stock, vinegar and puree. Bring to a boil, reduce heat, simmer, uncovered, about 1½ hours or until octopus is tender.

**3** Remove bay leaves, add oregano and sugar. Serve sprinkled with parsley.

**per serving** 9.9g total fat (1.9g saturated fat); 2178kJ (521 cal); 18.2g carbohydrate; 72.9g protein; 4.2g fibre

"I cook this quite often, and everyone loves it. It goes beautifully with a crisp salad and a little glass of ouzo."

Jan Purser (formerly Castorina) was chief home economist and then deputy food editor in the Test Kitchen for six years from 1987 to 1993. Jan helped plan and edit cookbooks, the menu planner series and the quick and easy series. She now lives in Perth, WA.

# mussels with beer

**PREPARATION TIME** 20 MINUTES  **COOKING TIME** 15 MINUTES  **SERVES** 4

1kg large mussels
1 tablespoon olive oil
2 cloves garlic, crushed
1 large red onion (300g), sliced thinly
2 fresh long red chillies, sliced thinly
1½ cups (375ml) beer
2 tablespoons sweet chilli sauce
1 cup coarsely chopped fresh flat-leaf parsley

GARLIC BREAD
1 loaf turkish bread (430g)
50g butter, melted
2 cloves garlic, crushed
2 tablespoons finely chopped fresh flat-leaf parsley

1 Scrub mussels; remove beards.
2 Make garlic bread.
3 Meanwhile, heat oil on heated barbecue flat plate (or grill plate or large frying pan); cook garlic, onion and chilli, stirring, until onion softens. Add mussels and combined beer and sauce; cook, covered, about 5 minutes or until mussels open (discard any that do not). Remove from heat; stir in parsley.
4 Serve mussels with garlic bread.
**garlic bread** Halve bread horizontally; cut each half into four pieces, brush with combined butter, garlic and parsley. Cook bread on heated oiled grill plate (or grill or barbecue), uncovered, until browned both sides.
**per serving** 19.7g total fat (8.3g saturated fat); 2129kJ (509 cal); 58.7g carbohydrate; 17.5g protein; 5.6g fibre

"I made these for my mum once and now they are a favourite at our house. The bread is great for soaking up juices."

Elizabeth Macri, a senior home economist, has been in the Test Kitchen for two years, developing and testing recipes, cooking for photography and helping the Test Kitchen manager.

"One of my favourite light summer lunches when entertaining my friends."

Margaret lentile worked in the Test Kitchen from 2001 to 2003, and was the chef for our in-house Test Kitchen catering. She has worked for respected cookery writer Maureen Simpson, and is now with a catering company.

# salmon cutlets with green apple salad

**PREPARATION TIME** 20 MINUTES  **COOKING TIME** 10 MINUTES (PLUS COOLING TIME)  **SERVES** 4

½ teaspoon sea salt

4 salmon cutlets (1kg)

2 medium green apples (300g), sliced thinly

2 green onions, sliced thinly

1 medium red onion (170g), sliced thinly

1½ cups loosely packed fresh mint leaves

¾ cup loosely packed fresh coriander leaves

½ cup (125ml) lemon juice

¾ cup (120g) roasted unsalted cashews

## PALM SUGAR DRESSING

⅓ cup (90g) grated palm sugar

2 tablespoons fish sauce

2cm piece fresh ginger (10g), grated

1 Combine ingredients for palm sugar dressing in small saucepan; bring to a boil. Remove from heat; strain. Cool to room temperature.

2 Sprinkle salt evenly over fish. Cook fish on heated oiled grill plate (or grill or barbecue) until browned and cooked as desired.

3 Combine apple, onions, mint, coriander and juice in large bowl; pour over half of the palm sugar dressing, toss to combine. Divide fish among serving plates; top with salad then cashews. Drizzle with remaining dressing.

**tips** You can also use ocean trout fillets in this recipe. Cooking times will change slightly for each different kind and thickness of fish you select. Salmon and ocean trout are at their best if slightly underdone.

Don't slice the apples until you are ready to toss the salad with the dressing because the flesh will brown when exposed to air.

**per serving** 29.5g total fat (5.8g saturated fat); 2157kJ (516 cal); 16g carbohydrate; 46.5g protein; 5.2g fibre

# paella

PREPARATION TIME 20 MINUTES (PLUS STANDING TIME)  COOKING TIME 1 HOUR 10 MINUTES
SERVES 8

Calasparra rice is a short-grain rice available from Spanish delicatessens
and gourmet-food stores. If you can't find calasparra, any short-grain rice
can be substituted.

1kg clams
1 tablespoon coarse cooking salt
1kg uncooked medium prawns
1kg small mussels
⅓ cup (80ml) olive oil
1.5 litres (6 cups) chicken or fish stock
1 large pinch saffron threads
4 chicken thigh fillets (440g), chopped coarsely
400g chorizo sausage, sliced thickly
2 large red onions (600g), chopped finely
2 medium red capsicums (400g), chopped finely
4 cloves garlic, crushed
1 tablespoon smoked paprika
4 medium tomatoes (600g), peeled, seeded, chopped finely
3 cups (600g) calasparra rice
2 cups (240g) frozen peas
¼ cup finely chopped fresh flat-leaf parsley

1 Rinse clams under cold water, place in large bowl with salt, cover with cold water,
stand 2 hours. Drain then rinse.

2 Shell and devein prawns, leaving tails intact. Reserve shells. Scrub mussels and
remove beards.

3 Heat 1 tablespoon of the oil in large saucepan; add prawn shells, cook, stirring,
until browned. Add stock, bring to a boil; simmer, uncovered, 20 minutes. Strain
through fine sieve into jug or bowl; add saffron to the liquid.

4 Heat another 1 tablespoon of the oil in 45cm paella pan or large non-stick frying
pan, add chicken; cook until browned all over, remove from pan. Add chorizo to
same pan, cook until browned all over; drain on absorbent paper.

5 Heat remaining oil in paella pan, add onion, capsicum, garlic, paprika and tomatoes;
cook, stirring, until soft. Add rice; stir to coat in mixture.

6 Add chicken, chorizo and stock to pan; stir until just combined. Do not stir again.
Bring mixture to a boil then simmer, uncovered, about 15 minutes or until the
rice is almost tender.

7 Sprinkle peas over rice; place clams, prawns and mussels evenly over surface
of paella. Cover pan with large sheets of foil; simmer about 5 minutes or until
mussels and clams have opened (discard any that do not) and prawns are just
cooked through. Sprinkle with parsley, serve immediately.

tips The traditional paella pan is shallow and wide. If you don't have a large
enough pan, use two smaller frying pans; the mixture is about 4cm deep.
A good-quality marinara mix could replace the seafood.

per serving  30.4g total fat (8.6g saturated fat); 3206kJ (767 cal); 72.3g carbohydrate;
51g protein; 4.7g fibre

"Since going to Spain
for a second time
some years ago, I've
become known for
my paella – this
was in the WW in
December 2003."

Lyndey Milan
joined the WW as food
director in 1999. She is also
co-host of TV's *Fresh with
The Australian Women's
Weekly,* on the Nine Network
in Australia and Prime in
New Zealand – and mother
of two grown children.

# vegetarian

# mixed dhal

PREPARATION TIME 15 MINUTES (PLUS STANDING TIME)  COOKING TIME 45 MINUTES  SERVES 4

½ cup (100g) yellow split peas
½ cup (100g) green split peas
½ cup (100g) red lentils
2 tablespoons ghee
2 teaspoons black mustard seeds
½ teaspoon black onion seeds
2 medium brown onions (300g), chopped coarsely
4 cloves garlic, crushed
4cm piece fresh ginger (20g), grated
1 tablespoon ground cumin
1 tablespoon ground coriander
1 teaspoon ground turmeric
1 teaspoon chilli powder
2 x 400g cans chopped tomatoes
2½ cups (625ml) vegetable stock
⅓ cup (80ml) cream
2 tablespoons coarsely chopped fresh coriander

1 Rinse peas under cold water; drain. Put peas in small bowl, cover with water; stand 30 minutes; drain.
2 Rinse lentils under cold water; drain.
3 Heat ghee in large heavy-based frying pan; cook seeds, stirring, until they start to pop. Add onion, garlic and ginger; cook, stirring, until onion is browned lightly.
4 Add ground spices; cook, stirring, until fragrant. Add peas, lentils, undrained tomatoes and stock; bring to a boil. Reduce heat; simmer, covered, about 30 minutes or until lentils are tender.
5 Add cream; stir over low heat until just heated through. Serve dahl sprinkled with chopped coriander.

tip Dhal can be prepared a day ahead; keep, covered, in refrigerator.

per serving 20.1g total fat (12g saturated fat); 1881kJ (450 cal); 45.7g carbohydrate; 22.7g protein; 12.6g fibre

"Inspired by a recent trip to India, this dhal is easy to make and worth buying authentic ingredients for."

Jodie Tilse
was one of a lively Test Kitchen team from 1994 to 1997. She then spent four years assisting Neil Perry develop menus for Qantas. She recently helped Kylie Kwong on her new cookbook. Jodie now has two children.

# supreme cottage loaf

PREPARATION TIME 1 HOUR (PLUS STANDING TIME)

COOKING TIME 50 MINUTES (PLUS REFRIGERATION TIME)  SERVES 8

23cm-round cottage bread loaf

2 large red capsicums (700g)

1 large eggplant (500g)

2 tablespoons coarse cooking salt

1 small kumara (250g)

1 large zucchini (150g)

cooking-oil spray

⅓ cup firmly packed fresh basil leaves

¾ cup (180g) ricotta

¼ cup (20g) coarsely grated parmesan

### SUN-DRIED TOMATO PUREE

1 cup (150g) sun-dried tomatoes in oil, drained

2 cloves garlic, crushed

¼ cup lightly packed fresh oregano leaves

1 tablespoon wholegrain mustard

¼ cup (60ml) olive oil

1 Make sun-dried tomato puree.

2 Cut a lid from top of loaf, remove soft bread from inside of loaf, leaving
2cm shell. Brush sun-dried tomato puree inside lid and bread shell.

3 Quarter capsicums, remove seeds and membranes. Roast under grill or in
very hot oven (240°C/220°C fan-forced), skin-side up, until skin blisters and
blackens. Cover capsicum pieces in plastic or paper 5 minutes, peel away skin.

4 Cut eggplant into 1.5cm slices, sprinkle all over with salt; stand 30 minutes.
Rinse eggplant under cold water; drain on absorbent paper.

5 Preheat grill. Cut kumara and zucchini into 5mm slices. Spray eggplant,
kumara and zucchini slices with oil; grill, in batches, until browned lightly.

6 Place kumara inside bread shell; top with basil leaves, capsicum, zucchini
combined cheeses and eggplant. Replace lid, wrap loaf completely in plastic
wrap, place on oven tray, top with another oven tray, weight with heavy cans;
refrigerate overnight.

7 Preheat oven to very hot (240°C/220°C fan-forced).

8 Discard plastic wrap; place loaf on oven tray. Bake about 5 minutes or until crisp.

**sun-dried tomato puree**  Blend or process tomatoes, garlic, oregano and
mustard until almost smooth. With motor operating, gradually add oil, in a thin
stream, until combined.

**tip**  Loaf must be made a day ahead and heated on day of serving.

**per serving**  13.3g total fat (3.2g saturated fat); 1413kJ (338 cal); 42g carbohydrate;
12.3g protein; 7.9g fibre

"I love the flavours,
it looks stunning
and I just love
stuffing all those
vegetables into that
crusty bread shell."

Nadia French
came to the Test Kitchen
as "the shopping girl". By
the time she left – to have
the first of three babies – she
was cooking for photography.
Today, she has a business
with Emma Braz (page 51).

# sicilian spaghetti

PREPARATION TIME 45 MINUTES  COOKING TIME 1 HOUR 45 MINUTES  SERVES 6

3 large eggplants (1.5kg)
cooking-oil spray
1 tablespoon olive oil
500g beef mince
1 large brown onion (200g), chopped finely
2 cloves garlic, crushed
400g can chopped tomatoes
½ teaspoon dried oregano
2 tablespoons tomato paste
250g spaghetti
1 cup (120g) frozen peas
¾ cup (90g) coarsely grated cheddar
1 cup (80g) coarsely grated parmesan
⅓ cup (35g) packaged breadcrumbs
1 tablespoon finely chopped fresh flat-leaf parsley

"I just love Italian food. This recipe tastes delicious, especially with pesto, and feeds an army of people."

Frances Neylon
was part of the Test Kitchen team during 1990, then ran her own catering business for many years. She still loves cooking, but now fundraises for a large hospital.

1 Cut eggplants into 3mm slices; spray slices well with oil. Cook eggplant, in single layer, in batches, over medium heat, in large frying pan until browned lightly on both sides.

2 Heat oil in same large frying pan. Add beef; cook, stirring, until browned all over. Add onion and garlic; cook, stirring, 2 minutes. Add undrained tomatoes, oregano and tomato paste, bring to a boil; reduce heat, simmer, uncovered, about 30 minutes or until liquid is reduced by half.

3 Meanwhile, cook pasta in large saucepan of boiling water until tender; drain.

4 Boil, steam or microwave peas until tender; drain.

5 Combine beef mixture with spaghetti, peas and cheeses.

6 Preheat oven to moderate (180°C/160°C fan-forced).

7 Grease deep 22cm-round cake pan; sprinkle half of the breadcrumbs evenly over base and side of pan. Place large slice of eggplant in centre of pan. Arrange large slices of eggplant, overlapping, over base of pan.

8 Arrange overlapping slices of eggplant round side of pan; choose slices that fit as close as possible to cover side of pan. Use spoonfuls of beef mixture to support the eggplant as you work. Spoon remaining beef mixture into centre, press firmly.

9 Arrange remaining slices of eggplant, overlapping each slice, to cover top of filling completely; sprinkle with remaining breadcrumbs.

10 Cook about 30 minutes or until golden brown. Stand 5 minutes before turning onto serving plate. Serve sprinkled with parsley.

tips Eggplant can be grilled or barbecued.
Recipe can be made a day ahead; keep, covered, in refrigerator.

per serving 19.5g total fat (8.6g saturated fat); 2165kJ (518 cal); 47g carbohydrate; 38.5g protein; 11.6g fibre

# ricotta gnocchi in fresh tomato sauce

**PREPARATION TIME** 10 MINUTES  **COOKING TIME** 20 MINUTES  **SERVES** 4

500g firm ricotta
1 cup (80g) finely grated parmesan
½ cup (75g) plain flour
2 eggs, beaten lightly
1 tablespoon olive oil
4 medium tomatoes (600g), chopped coarsely
6 green onions, sliced thinly
2 tablespoons coarsely chopped fresh oregano
2 tablespoons balsamic vinegar
2 tablespoons olive oil, extra
½ cup (40g) shaved parmesan

1  Bring large saucepan of water to a boil.
2  Meanwhile, combine ricotta, grated parmesan, flour, egg and oil in large bowl. Drop rounded tablespoons of mixture into boiling water; cook, without stirring, until gnocchi float to the surface. Remove from pan; drain, cover to keep warm.
3  Combine tomato, onion, oregano and vinegar in medium bowl.
4  Top warm gnocchi with tomato mixture, extra oil then shaved parmesan.
   **per serving**  40.5g total fat (18g saturated fat); 2362kJ (565 cal); 18.7g carbohydrate; 31.7g protein; 2.8g fibre

"This ricotta gnocchi is a favourite because it's like a summer version of potato gnocchi... really refreshing."

Alison Webb
is a qualified chef who joined the Test Kitchen in 2000. She left three years later, choosing another branch of the food industry – sales. However, she stresses that, "the love of food never leaves you".

# silver beet with spirali

**PREPARATION TIME** 15 MINUTES  **COOKING TIME** 15 MINUTES  **SERVES** 4

500g spirali pasta

⅓ cup (80ml) olive oil

1 clove garlic, crushed

½ small white onion (40g), chopped finely

½ small red capsicum (75g), chopped finely

90g piece coppa, chopped finely

1 fresh small red thai chilli, sliced thinly

8 medium silver beet leaves (640g), trimmed, shredded finely

2 tablespoons coarsely grated parmesan

1 Cook pasta in large saucepan of boiling water, uncovered, until just tender; drain.

2 Meanwhile, heat oil in medium frying pan, add garlic, onion, capsicum, coppa and chilli; cook, stirring, 2 minutes. Add silver beet; cook, stirring constantly, until silver beet wilts. Stir in cheese.

3 Combine pasta and silver beet mixture; mix well.

**tip** Recipe best made just before serving.

Coppa is salted and dried pork.

**per serving** 22.1g total fat (4g saturated fat); 2646kJ (633 cal); 87.1g carbohydrate; 20.5g protein; 5.8g fibre

"I make this often for my family – it's a great favourite, though I omit the chilli for the kids."

Jo Anne Calabria (nee Power) is a food editor, writer and food consultant. She worked in the Test Kitchen from 1985 until 1987, was a magazine food editor for 10 years and is now a food consultant.

# vegetarian lasagne

PREPARATION TIME 40 MINUTES (PLUS STANDING TIME)  COOKING TIME 1 HOUR 50 MINUTES
SERVES 6

2 medium eggplants (600g)
2 tablespoons coarse cooking salt
2 tablespoons olive oil
2 medium red capsicums (400g)
1½ cups (390g) bottled tomato pasta sauce
250g instant lasagne sheets
¾ cup (75g) coarsely grated mozzarella
½ cup (130g) pesto
½ cup (40g) finely grated parmesan

## WHITE SAUCE
60g butter
¼ cup (35g) plain flour
1½ cups (375ml) milk
½ cup (40g) finely grated parmesan

1 Oil 2-litre (8-cup) rectangular baking dish.
2 Cut eggplants into 1cm slices. Place in colander, sprinkle all over with salt; stand 30 minutes.
3 Preheat oven to moderately hot (200°C/180°C fan-forced).
4 Rinse eggplant under cold water; pat dry with absorbent paper. Brush eggplant with oil; place, in single layer, on oven trays. Roast about 40 minutes or until tender.
5 Meanwhile, quarter capsicums, remove seeds and membranes. Roast under grill, skin-side up, until skin blisters and blackens. Cover capsicum pieces with plastic or paper for 5 minutes; peel away skin, cut capsicum into thick strips.
6  Make white sauce.
7 Reduce oven temperature to moderate (180°C/160°C fan-forced).
8 Spread one-third of the pasta sauce into baking dish. Top with one-third of the lasagne sheets, another third of the sauce, half of the eggplant and half of the mozzarella; repeat layering, using another third of the lasagne sheets, remaining sauce, all of the capsicum, and remaining mozzarella, lasagne and eggplant. Spread pesto over eggplant; top with white sauce.
9 Bake, covered, 30 minutes; uncover, sprinkle lasagne with parmesan, bake further 30 minutes or until browned. Remove from oven; stand, uncovered, about 5 minutes before serving.
white sauce  Melt butter in small saucepan; add flour, stir over heat until bubbling and grainy. Remove pan from heat, gradually stir in milk; return to heat, stir until mixture boils and thickens. Remove pan from heat; stir in cheese.
tip  You can substitute zucchini, spinach or leek for the eggplant.
Each vegetable should be individually cooked before being layered.
per serving  33.8g total fat (14.4g saturated fat); 2537kJ (607 cal); 56.9g carbohydrate; 20.7g protein; 6.2g fibre

"This is a favourite with my family, and anyone else who has tried it. I like to serve it with garlic bread and salad."
Sharon Reeve
is the youngest member of the Test Kitchen. She started as a junior almost two years ago, and is now assistant food editor of *Woman's Day*.

# baked pumpkin and spinach risotto

**PREPARATION TIME** 15 MINUTES  **COOKING TIME** 35 MINUTES  **SERVES** 4

500g butternut pumpkin, chopped coarsely
2 tablespoons olive oil
1½ cups (375ml) chicken stock
1.25 litres (5 cups) water
1 large brown onion (200g), chopped coarsely
2 cloves garlic, crushed
2 cups (400g) arborio rice
½ cup (125ml) dry white wine
500g spinach, trimmed, chopped coarsely
½ cup (80g) pine nuts, toasted
½ cup (40g) coarsely grated parmesan
½ cup (125ml) cream

1 Preheat oven to hot (220°C/200°C fan-forced).
2 Combine pumpkin with half of the oil in baking dish. Bake, uncovered, about 20 minutes or until tender.
3 Meanwhile, combine stock and the water in large saucepan; bring to a boil. Reduce heat; simmer.
4 Heat remaining oil in large saucepan; cook onion and garlic, stirring, until onion is soft. Add rice; stir to coat in mixture. Add wine; stir until almost evaporated.
5 Stir in 1 cup (250ml) of the hot stock mixture; cook, stirring, over low heat until liquid is absorbed. Continue adding stock mixture, in 1-cup batches, stirring, until liquid is absorbed after each addition. Total cooking time should be about 30 minutes or until rice is just tender.
6 Add spinach, pine nuts, cheese and cream; cook, stirring, until spinach wilts. Gently stir in baked pumpkin.

**tips** Pumpkin can be baked three hours ahead. The risotto is best made just before serving.

**per serving** 41.6g total fat (13.8g saturated fat); 3490kJ (835 cal); 91.5g carbohydrate; 19.3g protein; 5.7g fibre

"I'm a big fan of risotto....especially this one!"

Laura O'Brien was food director Pamela Clark's personal assistant. Now working for a property developer in Dublin, she plans to study journalism.

"I like to cook this when friends come around. It's so quick and easy to make and always tastes delicious."

Louise Patniotis is the food editor who compiled the recipes in this book. After 18 years in the Test Kitchen, she "still loves it!" and works producing the WW mini and maxi cookbooks. She is married and the mother of two sons.

# bavette with prawns, peas lemon and dill

**PREPARATION TIME** 10 MINUTES  **COOKING TIME** 20 MINUTES  **SERVES** 4

375g bavette
2 tablespoons olive oil
1kg uncooked large king prawns, shelled, deveined
2 cloves garlic, crushed
1½ cups (180g) frozen peas
2 teaspoons finely grated lemon rind
6 green onions, sliced thinly
1 tablespoon coarsely chopped fresh dill
¼ cup (60ml) lemon juice

1 Cook pasta in large saucepan of boiling water, uncovered, until just tender; drain. Return to pan.
2 Meanwhile, heat half of the oil in large frying pan. Halve prawns; cook prawns and garlic, in batches, until prawns are just changed in colour. Cover to keep warm.
3 Place peas in same frying pan; cook, stirring, until heated through. Add rind, onion and dill; cook, stirring, until onion is just tender. Return prawns to pan with juice; stir until heated through. Toss prawn mixture and remaining oil into hot pasta.
**per serving**  15.7g total fat (2.3g saturated fat); 2441kJ (584 cal); 69.8g carbohydrate; 39.2g protein; 8g fibre

# saganaki prawn ravioli

**PREPARATION TIME** 50 MINUTES  **COOKING TIME** 20 MINUTES  **SERVES** 4

2 tablespoons olive oil
5 large tomatoes (1kg), seeded, chopped coarsely
4 cloves garlic, crushed
2 tablespoons finely chopped fresh lemon thyme
700g uncooked medium prawns
⅓ cup (80g) sour cream
1 teaspoon finely grated lemon rind
200g fetta, crumbled
40 wonton wrappers

1 Heat half of the oil in large saucepan; cook tomato, garlic and half of the thyme,
stirring, 2 minutes. Cover; cook over low heat 5 minutes.

2 Meanwhile, shell and devein prawns; chop prawn meat coarsely. Combine prawn meat
in medium bowl with sour cream, rind, 150g of the cheese and remaining thyme.

3 Centre tablespoons of mixture on half of the wrappers; brush edges with water.
Top with remaining wrappers, press together to seal.

4 Cook ravioli in large saucepan of boiling water, uncovered, until cooked. Drain; divide
ravioli among plates, top with hot tomato mixture, then remaining cheese and oil.

**per serving** 30.8g total fat (14.6g saturated fat); 2378kJ (569 cal); 36.9g carbohydrate;
35.6g protein; 5.1g fibre

# cannelloni

PREPARATION TIME 45 MINUTES  COOKING TIME 1 HOUR 45 MINUTES (PLUS STANDING TIME)
SERVES 6

18 cannelloni tubes
1¼ cups (125g) coarsely grated mozzarella
2 tablespoons coarsely grated parmesan

### TOMATO SAUCE

1 tablespoon olive oil
1 medium brown onion (150g), chopped finely
1 clove garlic
400g can chopped tomatoes
2 tablespoons tomato paste

### FILLING

2 tablespoons olive oil
1 medium brown onion (150g), chopped finely
1 clove garlic, crushed
500g beef mince
1 tablespoon finely chopped fresh oregano
1 tablespoon finely chopped fresh basil
2 teaspoons tomato paste
250g frozen spinach, thawed
1 egg, beaten lightly
¼ cup (60ml) cream

### BÉCHAMEL SAUCE

1 medium brown onion (150g), sliced thinly
4 black peppercorns
1 cup (250ml) milk
15g butter
1 tablespoon plain flour
½ cup (125ml) cream

"This dish is always
a hit at our typical
'Italian-style' family
get togethers."
Christina Martignago
came to the Test Kitchen as
a home economist, working
on the WW cookbooks and
magazine. Currently, she's
a vocational lecturer in a
hospitality college.

1 Make tomato sauce. Make filling. Make béchamel sauce.
2 Preheat oven to moderate (180°C/160°C fan-forced).
3 Place ¼ cup of the tomato sauce over base of shallow 3-litre (12-cup) ovenproof
   dish. Place filling inside cannelloni tubes using teaspoon.
4 Place tubes over tomato sauce. Top with béchamel sauce then remaining
   tomato sauce. Sprinkle with cheeses; cook, uncovered, about 30 minutes.
   **tomato sauce**  Heat oil in large frying pan; cook onion and garlic until onion
   is soft. Add undrained tomatoes and paste; simmer, covered, 10 minutes.
   **filling**  Heat oil in large saucepan; cook onion and garlic until onion is soft. Add
   beef; cook, stirring, until browned all over. Add herbs and paste; cook, uncovered,
   10 minutes. Add drained spinach; stir in combined egg and cream.
   **béchamel sauce**  Heat onion, peppercorns and milk in small saucepan. Cool
   5 minutes. Strain milk into small jug. Melt butter in small saucepan. Add flour; stir
   over heat 1 minute. Add milk; stir until sauce boils and thickens. Stir in cream.
   **per serving** 39.5g total fat (19g saturated fat); 2278kJ (545 cal); 15.5g carbohydrate;
   33g protein; 5.4g fibre

# pastitso

PREPARATION TIME 30 MINUTES  COOKING TIME 1 HOUR 45 MINUTES  SERVES 6

250g macaroni
2 eggs, beaten lightly
¾ cup (60g) coarsely grated parmesan
2 tablespoons stale breadcrumbs

### MEAT SAUCE
1 tablespoon olive oil
2 medium brown onions (300g), chopped finely
750g beef mince
400g can chopped tomatoes
⅓ cup (95g) tomato paste
½ cup (125ml) beef stock
¼ cup (60ml) dry white wine
½ teaspoon ground cinnamon
1 egg, beaten lightly

### TOPPING
90g butter
½ cup (75g) plain flour
3½ cups (875ml) milk
1 cup (80g) coarsely grated parmesan
2 egg yolks

"A favourite dish for entertaining large numbers — it's full of flavour and can be made in advance."

Kathy Snowball
was an assistant food editor in the Test Kitchen before joining *Australian Gourmet Traveller* as food editor. Kathy is part owner of a handmade biscuits and cakes business.

1 Preheat oven to moderate (180°C/160°C fan-forced). Grease shallow 2.5-litre (10-cup) ovenproof dish.
2 Meanwhile, add pasta to large saucepan of boiling water; boil, uncovered, until just tender, drain.
3 Combine warm pasta, egg and cheese in bowl; mix well. Press pasta over base of dish.
4 Make meat sauce. Make topping.
5 Top pasta evenly with meat sauce, pour over topping; smooth surface then sprinkle with breadcrumbs. Bake, uncovered, about 1 hour or until browned lightly. Stand 10 minutes before serving.

**meat sauce**  Heat oil in large saucepan, add onion; cook, stirring, until onion is soft. Add beef; cook, stirring, until beef is well browned. Stir in undrained tomatoes, tomato paste, stock, wine and cinnamon; simmer, uncovered, until thick. Cool 10 minutes; stir in egg.

**topping**  Melt butter in medium saucepan, add flour, stir over heat until bubbling. Remove from heat, gradually stir in milk. Stir over heat until sauce boils and thickens; stir in cheese. Cool 5 minutes; stir in egg yolks.

**tip**  Pastitso can be made a day ahead; keep, covered, in refrigerator; it is also suitable to freeze.

**per serving**  41.7g total fat (21.8g saturated fat); 3398kJ (813 cal); 54.4g carbohydrate; 54g protein; 3.8g fibre

## salads

# thai char-grilled beef salad

PREPARATION TIME 20 MINUTES (PLUS REFRIGERATION TIME)  COOKING TIME 15 MINUTES
SERVES 4

600g piece beef rump steak
2 teaspoons sesame oil
⅓ cup (80ml) kecap manis
1 cup loosely packed fresh mint leaves
1 cup loosely packed fresh coriander leaves
½ cup loosely packed fresh thai basil leaves
6 green onions, sliced thinly
5 shallots (125g), sliced thinly
250g cherry tomatoes, halved
1 telegraph cucumber (400g), seeded, sliced thinly
10 kaffir lime leaves, shredded finely
100g mesclun

### SWEET AND SOUR DRESSING
½ cup (125ml) lime juice
¼ cup (60ml) fish sauce
2 teaspoons white sugar
2 fresh small red thai chillies, sliced thinly

1 Place beef in shallow dish; brush all over with combined oil and kecap manis.
Cover; refrigerate 30 minutes.
2 Meanwhile, combine herbs, onion, shallot, tomato and cucumber in large bowl;
toss gently.
3 Combine ingredients for sweet and sour dressing in screw-top jar; shake well.
4 Cook beef on heated oiled grill plate (or grill or barbecue) until browned lightly
and cooked as desired. Cover beef; stand 10 minutes then slice thinly.
5 Place beef, lime leaves and mesclun in large bowl with herb mixture. Add sweet
and sour dressing; toss gently to combine.
tips Thai basil, also known as horapa, has small leaves, purplish stems and a
sweet licorice flavour; it is one of the basic flavours that typify Thai cuisine.
Rib-eye, boneless sirloin or eye fillet steaks are all good substitutes for rump in
this recipe.
per serving 11.7g total fat (4.1g saturated fat); 1225kJ (293 cal); 8.8g carbohydrate;
37g protein; 4.3g fibre

"The fresh but spicy
tastes of coriander,
mint and kaffir lime
blend beautifully with
the barbecued beef."

Belinda Black
began by baking pies for a
shop on Sydney's northern
beaches. She graduated to
restaurants then, to escape
night shifts, joined the Test
Kitchen for six months. She
now cooks for private clients.

# avocado and artichoke salad

**PREPARATION TIME** 15 MINUTES (PLUS REFRIGERATION TIME) **SERVES** 4

1 medium avocado (250g), sliced
8 bottled artichoke hearts in oil, drained, quartered
2 lebanese cucumbers (260g), sliced thinly
1 small mignonette lettuce, torn

**LIME AND BASIL VINAIGRETTE**
¼ cup (60ml) olive oil
¼ cup (60ml) lime juice
1 fresh small red thai chilli, chopped finely
1 tablespoon finely shredded fresh basil
½ teaspoon white sugar

1 Combine ingredients for lime and basil vinaigrette in screw-top jar; shake well.
2 Combine avocado, artichoke and cucumber in medium bowl, add vinaigrette; cover, refrigerate 2 hours.
3 Place lettuce in bowl. Serve avocado mixture over lettuce.
**per serving** 24.1g total fat (4.1g saturated fat); 1028kJ (246 cal); 3.6g carbohydrate; 3.8g protein; 5.2g fibre

"This recipe reminds me of summer. It's quick, easy and I sometimes add prawns for a treat."

Sue Geraghty (nee Hipwell) worked in the Test Kitchen from 1986 to 1990, then turned to freelance recipe development and testing kitchen appliances. Now, she's studying science.

# smoked chicken and pear salad

PREPARATION TIME 15 MINUTES  SERVES 4

150g radicchio lettuce, torn
100g mignonette lettuce, torn
200g smoked cooked chicken, sliced thinly
1 large pear (330g), sliced thinly
1 medium red onion (170g), sliced thinly
¼ cup (60ml) red wine vinegar
1 tablespoon balsamic vinegar
⅓ cup (80ml) olive oil
¼ teaspoon white sugar

1 Combine lettuces, chicken, pear and onion in large bowl.
2 Combine the remaining ingredients in a screw-top jar; shake well.
3 Drizzle dressing over lettuce mixture; toss gently to combine.

**tips** The dressing can be made a day ahead.

The recipe is best assembled just before serving.

You can use a store-bought barbecue chicken in this recipe, if preferred.

**per serving** 21.9g total fat (3.6g saturated fat); 1262kJ (302 cal); 12.7g carbohydrate; 13.8g protein; 3.1g fibre

"Light, fresh flavours that marry up well – it's yummy!"

Allyson Quaratino (nee Mitchell) was a junior home economist at the Test Kitchen in 1985 (after doing work experience in the Test Kitchen while studying at TAFE). She is now in a sales position, and the mother of a daughter.

# warm balmain bug salad with saffron dressing

PREPARATION TIME 30 MINUTES  COOKING TIME 10 MINUTES  SERVES 4

24 uncooked balmain bugs (4.8kg)
500g cherry tomatoes
2 large avocados (640g), sliced thinly
1 medium red onion (170g), sliced thinly
80g snow pea tendrils
½ cup firmly packed fresh basil leaves

SAFFRON DRESSING
8 saffron threads
¼ cup (60ml) boiling water
1 egg yolk
1 clove garlic, crushed
1 teaspoon english mustard
2 tablespoons lemon juice
½ cup (125ml) light olive oil

1 Make saffron dressing.

2 Meanwhile, place each bug, upside down, on chopping board; cut tail from body. Discard body; cut through tail lengthways, remove and discard vein. Remove meat from both tail halves.

3 Cook meat and tomatoes, in batches, on heated oiled grill plate (or grill or barbecue) until browned all over.

4 Just before serving, combine tomatoes, avocado, onion, tendrils and basil in large bowl with one-third of the saffron dressing. Divide salad mixture among serving plates; top with meat, drizzle with remaining dressing.

saffron dressing  Combine saffron and the water in small heatproof bowl; stand 10 minutes. Strain through fine strainer into small bowl; discard threads. Whisk egg yolk, garlic, mustard and juice in small bowl; gradually add oil, in thin stream, whisking continuously. Whisk in saffron liquid.

tips  Slice avocado just before assembling the salad.

You can substitute prawns or lobster for the balmain bugs, if you prefer.

You can use opal basil leaves, instead of the sweet leaves, if preferred.

Tomatoes can be browned on an oven tray under a grill or in a hot oven.

This recipe can be made with cooked balmain bugs, if uncooked are unavailable. Reheat meat under grill until just warm, if desired.

per serving  58.8g total fat (10.7g saturated fat); 3804kJ (910 cal); 10.5g carbohydrate; 85.3g protein; 5.4g fibre

# festive chicken salad

**PREPARATION TIME** 30 MINUTES  **COOKING TIME** 55 MINUTES (PLUS COOLING TIME)
**SERVES** 6

1.8kg chicken
1 cup (250ml) soy sauce
1 cup (250ml) water
¼ cup (55g) white sugar
1 teaspoon sesame oil
1 teaspoon five-spice powder
2cm piece fresh ginger (10g), sliced
1 clove garlic, crushed
500g broccoli, chopped coarsely
1 medium red capsicum (200g), sliced
410g can baby corn, drained
3 green onions, sliced

### GINGER DRESSING
⅓ cup (80ml) peanut oil
2 teaspoons honey
2 teaspoons white vinegar
1 teaspoon soy sauce
4cm piece fresh ginger (20g), grated

1 Rinse chicken, pat dry with absorbent paper inside and out. Combine sauce, the water, sugar, oil, five-spice, ginger and garlic in large saucepan. Add chicken, bring to a boil, uncovered. Reduce heat, cover; simmer, about 40 minutes or until cooked, turning once. Remove from heat; stand chicken in covered saucepan until cold. Drain chicken; remove meat from bones; slice meat.

2 Boil, steam or microwave broccoli until tender; drain, rinse under cold water, drain.

3 Meanwhile, combine ingredients for ginger dressing in screw-top jar; shake well.

4 Combine chicken, broccoli, capsicum, corn and onion in large bowl. Pour dressing over salad just before serving.

**tip** Cook chicken, allow time to cool and serve on the same day, if possible. Use a saucepan just large enough to hold the chicken.

**per serving** 37.7g total fat (9.9g saturated fat); 2383kJ (570 cal); 21.7g carbohydrate; 36.7g protein; 4.2g fibre

"An Asian-flavoured salad, this suits any occasion; it's so popular with my sailing friends."

Jacqui Hudson (nee Hing) has been a freelance food stylist for around 20 years – and was one of the first food stylists for the WW cookbooks. She now styles food for TV, is a mother of three and is studying fine arts.

# accompaniments

"I like this for its versatility; serve it as a bruschetta topping or as an accompaniment to meat or seafood."

Angela Bresnahan worked in the Test Kitchen from 1992 to 1994, moved on to Queensland's Whitsunday Islands, then overseas for five years. She owned and ran a cafe and restaurant, and is now a head chef.

## caponata

**PREPARATION TIME** 15 MINUTES
**COOKING TIME** 20 MINUTES (PLUS COOLING AND STANDING TIME) **SERVES** 6

2 medium red capsicums (400g)
3 trimmed celery stalks (300g)
2 small red onions (200g)
2 medium tomatoes (300g)
2 medium eggplants (600g)
1 tablespoon olive oil
1 clove garlic, chopped finely
cooking-oil spray
½ cup (110g) white sugar
1 cup (250ml) red wine vinegar
½ cup (80g) sultanas
100g seeded black olives
⅓ cup (50g) pine nuts, toasted
1½ tablespoons capers, rinsed, drained

1 Cut capsicums, celery, onions, tomatoes and eggplants into 2cm pieces.
2 Heat oil in large frying pan, cook capsicum, celery, onion, tomato and garlic, in batches, until soft; transfer to large bowl.
3 Spray eggplant all over with oil, cook eggplant in batches, until browned. Add to capsicum mixture.
4 Place sugar in medium frying pan over low heat. Cook, without stirring or boiling, until dissolved, swirling pan occasionally. Cook about 5 minutes or until browned lightly. Add vinegar, bring to a boil; reduce heat, simmer, uncovered, until liquid is reduced by a third; cool to room temperature.
5 Add vinegar mixture to vegetables with sultanas, olives, nuts and capers; stir until combined. Stand for 1 hour at room temperature before serving.
**tip** This recipe can be made a day ahead.
**per serving** 10g total fat (0.8g saturated fat); 1137kJ (272 cal); 40.6g carbohydrate; 4.9g protein; 6.1g fibre

# crunchy fried noodle coleslaw

**PREPARATION TIME** 35 MINUTES  **SERVES** 8

10 trimmed radishes (150g)
1 large red capsicum (350g), sliced thinly
1 small chinese cabbage (700g), shredded finely
6 green onions, sliced thinly
1 cup (80g) bean sprouts
½ cup (70g) slivered almonds, toasted
2 x 100g packets fried noodles

### SWEET-SOUR DRESSING
⅔ cup (160ml) peanut oil
2 tablespoons white vinegar
2 tablespoons brown sugar
2 tablespoons soy sauce
2 teaspoons sesame oil
1 clove garlic, crushed

1 Slice radishes into matchstick-size pieces. Combine radish in large bowl with capsicum, cabbage, onion, sprouts, nuts and noodles.
2 Combine ingredients for sweet-sour dressing in screw-top jar; shake well.
3 Pour sweet-sour dressing over salad; toss to combine.
**per serving** 24.3g total fat (3.7g saturated fat); 1087kJ (260 cal); 6.8g carbohydrate; 4.2g protein; 3g fibre

"This salad is always a crowd pleaser... you don't have to go to great lengths to make something different for your family and friends."

Alison Webb
is a qualified chef who joined the Test Kitchen in 2000. She left three years later, choosing another branch of the food industry – sales. However, she stresses that, "the love of food never leaves you".

# sumac wedges

PREPARATION TIME 5 MINUTES  COOKING TIME 25 MINUTES  SERVES 4

Sumac, a granular spice ranging in colour from terracotta to almost-black purple, is used extensively from the eastern Mediterranean through to Pakistan. Its tart astringency adds a delightful piquancy to food without the heat of chilli. Available from Middle Eastern food stores.

1kg sebago potatoes, washed
2 tablespoons sumac
2 tablespoons olive oil

1 Preheat oven to very hot (240°C/220°C fan-forced). Lightly grease oven tray.
2 Cut potatoes into wedges; combine in large microwave-safe bowl with sumac and oil.
3 Cook, covered, in microwave oven, on HIGH (100%), 5 minutes.
4 Place wedges, in single layer, on tray. Roast about 20 minutes or until wedges are crisp. Sprinkle with sea salt flakes, if desired.
   **per serving**  9.3g total fat (1.3g saturated fat); 915kJ (219 cal); 28.1g carbohydrate; 5.1g protein; 4.3g fibre

"With hubby's and my own busy lifestyles, I find these are easy and delicious with any meal."

Kellie McChesney (nee Ann) spent 2001 and 2002 in the Test Kitchen, half that time as senior home economist. She now works with a partner in their new Sydney-based food product business.

# potato crush

PREPARATION TIME 10 MINUTES  COOKING TIME 15 MINUTES  SERVES 6

1kg tiny new potatoes, unpeeled
½ cup (120g) sour cream
40g butter, softened

1 Boil, steam or microwave potatoes until tender; drain.
2 Mash half of the potatoes with all the sour cream and butter in large bowl.
3 Stir in one of the flavour variations (below).
4 Using back of a fork or potato masher, gently crush remaining potatoes until skins burst and flesh is just flattened; fold into mash mixture.

### ORIGINAL POTATO CRUSH

Combine 6 coarsely chopped drained cornichons, 3 coarsely chopped green onions, ¼ cup coarsely chopped fresh flat-leaf parsley and 1 tablespoon coarsely chopped drained capers in small bowl. Add to Step 3, above.

**per serving** 13.7g total fat (8.8g saturated fat); 1116kJ (267 cal); 30.7g carbohydrate; 4.8g protein; 4.3g fibre

### CAESAR CRUSH

Cook 3 finely chopped bacon rashers in non-stick frying pan until crisp; drain on absorbent paper. Combine with 4 finely chopped anchovies, 1 crushed garlic clove, 3 thinly sliced green onions and ½ cup shaved parmesan in small bowl. Add to Step 3, above.

**per serving** 17.6g total fat (10.9g saturated fat); 1246kJ (298 cal); 23g carbohydrate; 11.6g protein; 3.5g fibre

### HERB AND MUSTARD CRUSH

Combine 1 tablespoon wholegrain mustard, ¼ cup coarsely chopped fresh chives, ¼ cup coarsely chopped fresh flat-leaf parsley, 2 tablespoons coarsely chopped fresh basil and 2 tablespoons coarsely chopped fresh dill in small bowl. Add to Step 3, above.

**per serving** 13.7g total fat (8.8g saturated fat); 978kJ (234 cal); 22.8g carbohydrate; 4.7g protein; 3.6g fibre

"This tastes just as good cold as hot; my son Max loves it with bacon, shallots and cheese in it."

Myles Beaufort
was a Test Kitchen member from 1993 to 1994, then a freelance food stylist. In 1996, his own book was published and, in 1997, he presented a 5-minute recipe segment on Foxtel FX TV. He and his family live in Queensland.

ORIGINAL POTATO CRUSH

## asparagus with anchovies and garlic

PREPARATION TIME 5 MINUTES   COOKING TIME 5 MINUTES   SERVES 2

200g asparagus, trimmed
2 tablespoons extra virgin olive oil
1 clove garlic, sliced thinly
3 anchovies, drained, chopped coarsely

1 Preheat oven to moderately hot (200°C/180°C fan-forced).
2 Place asparagus in shallow baking dish; pour over combined oil, garlic
  and anchovies. Toss asparagus to coat in the oil mixture.
3 Roast about 5 minutes or until asparagus is just tender.
  **per serving**  18.8g total fat (2.7g saturated fat); 786kJ (188 cal); 1.6g carbohydrate;
  3.8g protein; 1.8g fibre

## asparagus with butter and parmesan

PREPARATION TIME 5 MINUTES   COOKING TIME 5 MINUTES   SERVES 2

200g asparagus, trimmed
20g butter, melted
2 tablespoons parmesan flakes

1 Bring water to a boil in large saucepan; add asparagus, simmer, uncovered,
  about 5 minutes or until just tender.
2 Serve asparagus drizzled with melted butter and sprinkled with parmesan.
  **per serving**  10.6g total fat (6.9g saturated fat); 506kJ (121 cal); 1.5g carbohydrate;
  5.2g protein; 1.5g fibre

## asparagus with balsamic dressing

PREPARATION TIME 5 MINUTES   COOKING TIME 5 MINUTES   SERVES 2

200g asparagus, trimmed
2 tablespoons extra virgin olive oil
3 teaspoons balsamic vinegar
1 medium tomato (150g), peeled, seeded, chopped finely
1 tablespoon small basil leaves

1 Cook asparagus on heated, lightly oiled grill plate (or grill on barbecue) about
  5 minutes or until tender.
2 Serve drizzled with combined oil, vinegar and tomato; sprinkle with basil leaves.
  **per serving**  18.4g total fat (2.6g saturated fat); 790kJ (189 cal); 2.8g carbohydrate;
  3.3g protein; 2.5g fibre

"The asparagus looks gorgeous on a big white platter, served as a starter or with seafood, veal cutlets or chicken."

Frances Abdallaoui is the WW's deputy food editor. She joined the magazine in 1999, after being part of the Test Kitchen team during 1993 to 1994. Fran is married with two children.

# desserts

The part of a meal that leaves a lasting impression

# superb sour cream cheesecake

**PREPARATION TIME** 30 MINUTES (PLUS REFRIGERATION TIME)
**COOKING TIME** 50 MINUTES (PLUS COOLING TIME) **SERVES** 8

250g packet plain sweet biscuits
150g butter, melted
250g packet cream cheese, softened
250g cottage cheese
3 eggs
1 cup (220g) caster sugar
2 tablespoons cornflour
½ cup (125ml) milk
1 cup (240g) sour cream
1 tablespoon finely grated lemon rind
1 teaspoon lemon juice

1 Preheat oven to moderately slow (170°C/150°C fan-forced).

2 Blend or process biscuits until mixture resembles fine breadcrumbs. Add butter; process until combined. Press biscuit mixture evenly over base and side of 20cm springform tin, place on oven tray; refrigerate about 30 minutes or until firm.

3 Meanwhile, beat cheeses together until smooth. Beat in eggs, one at a time. Stir in sugar and cornflour then milk, cream, rind and juice; pour into crumb crust.

4 Bake about 50 minutes. Cool in oven with door ajar. Refrigerate overnight.

**per serving** 45.3g total fat (28.1g saturated fat); 2704kJ (54.5 cal); 54.5g carbohydrate; 8.5g protein; 0.7g fibre

"My favourite recipe is this one that my mum used to make, and my sister and I still use for dinners and parties."

Naomi Scesny worked in the Test Kitchen from 2000 to 2001. She is now a full-time home economist for a commercial company specialising in small appliances.

# lemon cheesecake

**PREPARATION TIME** 30 MINUTES (PLUS REFRIGERATION TIME) **SERVES** 8

250g packet plain sweet biscuits
125g butter, melted
250g packet cream cheese, softened
395g can sweetened condensed milk
2 teaspoons finely grated lemon rind
⅓ cup (80ml) lemon juice
1 teaspoon gelatine
1 tablespoon water

1 Blend or process biscuits until mixture resembles fine breadcrumbs. Add butter; process until combined. Press biscuit mixture evenly over base and side of 20cm springform tin, place on tray; refrigerate about 30 minutes or until firm.

2 Meanwhile, beat cream cheese in small bowl with electric mixer until smooth. Beat in condensed milk, rind and juice; beat until smooth.

3 Sprinkle gelatine over the water in small heatproof jug; stand jug in small saucepan of simmering water. Stir until gelatine dissolves; cool 5 minutes.

4 Stir gelatine mixture into lemon mixture. Pour mixture into crumb crust; cover cheesecake; refrigerate about 3 hours or until set.

**tip** This recipe can be made a day ahead; keep, covered, in refrigerator.

**per serving** 32.8g total fat (20.5g saturated fat); 2186kJ (523 cal); 50.3g carbohydrate; 9.2g protein; 0.7g fibre

"My mum makes this cheesecake, it's the best in the whole world. Made with love, and served with fresh cream, it is special."

Nicole Jennings has a degree in Applied Science – Food and Nutrition and is studying to be a chef. A home economist in the Test Kitchen, she works on both the WW cookbooks and magazine.

# sticky date pudding with butterscotch sauce

**PREPARATION TIME** 35 MINUTES  **COOKING TIME** 1 HOUR 5 MINUTES  **SERVES** 6

1¾ cups (250g) coarsely chopped seeded dates
1¼ cups (310ml) water
1 teaspoon bicarbonate of soda
60g butter
¾ cup (165g) caster sugar
2 eggs
1 cup (150g) self-raising flour

**BUTTERSCOTCH SAUCE**
1 cup (220g) firmly packed brown sugar
1 cup (250ml) cream
200g butter

1 Preheat oven to moderate (180°C/160°C fan-forced). Grease deep 20cm-round cake pan; line base with baking paper.

2 Combine dates and the water in medium saucepan, bring to a boil; remove from heat, add soda, stand 5 minutes. Blend or process mixture until smooth.

3 Beat butter, sugar and one of the eggs in small bowl with electric mixer until light and fluffy. Beat in remaining egg. (Mixture will curdle at this stage, but will come together later.) Stir in sifted flour then date mixture.

4 Pour mixture into pan; bake about 55 minutes. Stand pudding 10 minutes before turning onto wire rack over oven tray; turn pudding top-side up.

5 Meanwhile, make butterscotch sauce.

6 Pour ¼ cup sauce over pudding. Return pudding to moderate oven; bake, uncovered, further 5 minutes. Serve pudding with remaining sauce.

**butterscotch sauce** Combine ingredients in medium saucepan; stir over heat, without boiling, until sugar is dissolved. Simmer 3 minutes.

**tip** Pudding can be made four days ahead; keep, covered, in refrigerator. Reheat single servings in microwave oven on HIGH (100%) for about 30 seconds just before serving.

**per serving** 55.8g total fat (36g saturated fat); 3879kJ (928 cal); 105.7g carbohydrate; 6.5g protein; 4.4g fibre

"This scrumptious pudding was such a hit at our food tasting, everyone was coming back for seconds."

Carolyn Fienberg came to the Test Kitchen as a home economist in 1976, detoured to London's Cordon Bleu school, and returned to be food editor and food stylist on a number of lifestyle magazines.

# tarte tatin

PREPARATION TIME 30 MINUTES (PLUS REFRIGERATION TIME)
COOKING TIME 45 MINUTES (PLUS COOLING TIME) SERVES 6

2 tablespoons orange juice
⅔ cup (150g) caster sugar
70g butter
3 medium apples (450g), peeled

PASTRY
1 cup (150g) plain flour
80g cold butter, chopped
1 tablespoon caster sugar
1 tablespoon cold water, approximately

1 Combine juice, sugar and butter in 23cm heavy-based ovenproof frying pan; stir over heat, without boiling, until sugar is dissolved. Simmer, stirring occasionally, until mixture becomes a thick, light golden caramel. Remove from heat.

2 Halve apples; cut each half into three wedges, remove cores. Pack apple wedges, rounded-sides down, tightly into pan over caramel, return to heat; simmer, uncovered, about 15 minutes or until most of the liquid is evaporated and caramel is dark golden brown. Remove from heat; cool 1 hour.

3 Meanwhile, make pastry.

4 Preheat oven to moderate (180°C/160°C fan-forced).

5 Roll pastry into circle a little larger than the frying pan. Lift pastry, without stretching it, on top of apples, tuck inside edge of pan. Bake about 25 minutes or until pastry is golden brown and crisp. Remove tarte from oven, stand 5 minutes.

6 Carefully invert tarte onto plate. Serve warm with cream, if desired.

pastry Blend or process flour, butter and sugar until mixture resembles fine breadcrumbs. Add enough water to make ingredients just cling together. Knead dough on floured surface until smooth. Cover, refrigerate 1 hour.

tips Golden delicious apples will give you the best results in this recipe.
Apple caramel mixture and pastry can be made a day ahead; store separately, covered, in the refrigerator.

per serving 20.9g total fat (13.6g saturated fat); 1689kJ (404 cal); 53.1g carbohydrate; 3.1g protein; 2g fibre

# almond pear flan

PREPARATION TIME 30 MINUTES (PLUS REFRIGERATION TIME)  COOKING TIME 35 MINUTES
SERVES 8

1 ¼ cups (185g) plain flour
90g cold butter, chopped
¼ cup (55g) caster sugar
2 egg yolks
125g butter, softened, extra
⅓ cup (75g) caster sugar, extra
2 eggs
1 tablespoon plain flour, extra
1 cup (120g) almond meal
3 medium pears (690g), peeled, cored, quartered
2 tablespoons apricot jam

1 Preheat oven to moderate (180°C/160°C fan-forced).
2 Process flour, butter, sugar and egg yolks until combined. Transfer to lightly
   floured surface, knead into a smooth ball; cover, refrigerate pastry 30 minutes.
3 Beat extra butter and extra sugar until combined; beat in eggs and extra flour
   until combined. Stir in almond meal.
4 Roll pastry to line 22cm-round loose-based flan tin. Spread almond mixture into
   pastry case, top with pear. Bake about 35 minutes. Brush with warmed sieved jam.
   **per serving**  33.4g total fat (15.9g saturated fat); 2161kJ (517 cal); 48g carbohydrate;
   8.5g protein; 3.5g fibre

"Every summer, using the mangoes from the huge old tree in my backyard, and with help from my two sons, I make this sorbet."

Louise Patniotis is the food editor who compiled the recipes in this book. After 18 years in the Test Kitchen, she "still loves it!" and works producing the WW mini and maxi cookbooks. She is married and the mother of two sons.

# mango sorbet

PREPARATION TIME 20 MINUTES  COOKING TIME 8 MINUTES (PLUS COOLING AND FREEZING TIME)
SERVES 6

1 cup (220g) white sugar
1 cup (250ml) water
⅓ cup (80ml) lemon juice
4 medium mangoes (1.7kg), peeled, chopped coarsely
2 egg whites, beaten lightly

1 Combine sugar and the water in medium saucepan. Stir over medium heat, without boiling, until sugar dissolves; add juice. Bring to a boil; reduce heat. Simmer, uncovered, 5 minutes; cool lemon syrup to room temperature.
2 Blend or process mango until smooth. Add lemon syrup and egg whites; process until combined.
3 Pour mixture into freezer-proof container. Cover; freeze until sorbet is just firm. Chop sorbet; process mixture until smooth. Return sorbet to container. Cover; freeze until firm.

tips For best results use fresh mango. You will need about 3½ cups mango puree for this recipe. Mango sorbet can be made a week ahead. Sorbet can also be made using an ice-cream maker, following the manufacturer's instructions.

per serving 0.4g total fat (0.0g saturated fat); 1095kJ (262 cal); 62.4g carbohydrate; 3.3g protein; 3g fibre

# fresh figs in honey and fennel syrup served with muscat granita

PREPARATION TIME 15 MINUTES  COOKING TIME 10 MINUTES (PLUS FREEZING TIME)  SERVES 4

1 cup (250ml) water
½ cup (125ml) muscat
½ cup (110g) caster sugar
1 teaspoon black peppercorns
1 teaspoon finely grated lemon rind
1 tablespoon lemon juice
1 tablespoon fennel seeds
½ cup (125ml) water, extra
¼ cup (90g) honey
8 large fresh figs (640g)

1 Combine the water, muscat, sugar, peppercorns, rind and juice in small saucepan; bring to a boil. Cool 10 minutes; strain into 14cm x 21cm loaf pan. Cover with foil; freeze about 4 hours or until firm, scraping granita from bottom and sides of pan with fork every hour.

2 Dry-fry fennel seeds in small saucepan until fragrant. Add the extra water and honey; bring to a boil. Reduce heat; simmer, uncovered, without stirring, about 5 minutes or until mixture thickens slightly. Strain through sieve into small jug; discard seeds. Cool syrup 10 minutes.

3 Cut figs lengthways into five slices; divide among serving plates, drizzle with syrup, top with granita.

tip Muscat is a sweet, aromatic dessert wine, possessing an almost musty flavour. It is made from the fully-matured muscatel grape. Tokay, sweet riesling or gewürztraminer can be substituted for the muscat in the granita; drink what remains of the wine with this dessert.

per serving 0.5g total fat (0.0g saturated fat); 1216kJ (291 cal); 62.9g carbohydrate; 2.4g protein; 4g fibre

"The combination of flavours in the granita are unexpected; perfect with fresh figs."

Jane Hann
has worked on the WW cookbooks as a freelance food stylist since 1991, and been part of the evolving look of the pages. She now juggles food styling with raising three sons.

# raspberry nougat frozen parfait

**PREPARATION TIME** 20 MINUTES (PLUS FREEZING AND REFRIGERATION TIME)
**COOKING TIME** 5 MINUTES  **SERVES** 8

2 cups (400g) ricotta
¾ cup (165g) caster sugar
300ml thickened cream
¼ cup (40g) whole almonds, toasted, chopped
150g nougat, chopped
1 cup (135g) frozen raspberries

### BERRY COMPOTE
2½ cups (330g) frozen raspberries
¼ cup (55g) caster sugar
500g fresh raspberries

1 Line 14cm x 21cm loaf pan with a strip of foil or baking paper to cover the base and extend 5cm over two long sides.
2 Blend or process ricotta and sugar until smooth. Beat cream in small bowl with electric mixer until soft peaks form. Combine ricotta mixture, nuts and nougat in large bowl; fold in cream, then raspberries.
3 Spoon mixture into pan, cover with foil; freeze until firm.
4 Slice parfait, then refrigerate about 30 minutes before serving, to soften slightly.
5 Meanwhile, make berry compote. Serve frozen parfait with berry compote.

**berry compote**  Combine frozen raspberries and sugar in medium saucepan; cook, stirring, over low heat, until berries are very soft. Push raspberry mixture through coarse sieve into medium bowl; discard seeds. Just before serving, combine raspberry puree and fresh berries in medium bowl.

**tips**  You can serve fresh berries instead of the berry compote, if preferred. The berry compote can be prepared a day ahead; keep, covered, in the refrigerator. The parfait can be made a week ahead up to step 3; slice with a knife that has been dipped in hot water, before allowing to soften in the refrigerator (step 4).

**per serving**  24.3g total fat (13.1g saturated fat); 1894kJ (453 cal); 50.5g carbohydrate; 9.3g protein; 7.1g fibre

"In summer, I serve this with poached peaches and, in the cooler months, with poached pears; it's versatile and no-fail."

Alexandra Elliott (nee McCowan) worked in the Test Kitchen for 11 years before leaving to become the WW's food editor, and a key member of the 2001 World Food Media Awards, and the 2003 Vittoria Food Media Awards winning team. She has special qualifications in coffee, olive oil tasting and cheese judging.

# cassata

PREPARATION TIME 1 HOUR (PLUS FREEZING TIME)  SERVES 8

2 eggs, separated
½ cup (80g) icing sugar
½ cup (125ml) cream
few drops almond essence

## SECOND LAYER
2 eggs, separated
½ cup (80g) icing sugar
½ cup (125ml) cream
60g dark eating chocolate, melted
2 tablespoons cocoa powder
1½ tablespoons water

## THIRD LAYER
1 cup (250ml) cream
1 teaspoon vanilla extract
1 egg white, beaten lightly
⅓ cup (55g) icing sugar
2 tablespoons red glacé cherries, chopped finely
2 glacé apricots, chopped finely
2 glacé pineapple rings, chopped finely
1 tablespoon green glacé cherries, chopped finely
30g flaked almonds, toasted

1 Beat egg whites in small bowl with electric mixer until firm peaks form; gradually beat in sifted icing sugar. Fold in lightly beaten egg yolks.
2 Beat cream and almond essence in small bowl with electric mixer until soft peaks form; fold into egg mixture. Pour mixture into deep 20cm-round cake pan. Level top; freeze until firm.
3 Make second layer and spread over almond layer; freeze until firm.
4 Make third layer and spread over second layer; freeze until firm.
5 Run small spatula around edge of cassata; wipe hot cloth over base and side of pan. Turn cassata onto serving plate.

**second layer**  Beat egg whites in small bowl with electric mixer until firm peaks form; gradually beat in sifted icing sugar. Beat cream in small bowl until soft peaks form; fold into egg white mixture. Place chocolate in small bowl; stir in egg yolks. Stir blended cocoa and water into chocolate mixture; fold chocolate mixture through cream mixture.

**third layer**  Beat cream and extract in small bowl with electric mixer until firm peaks form. Beat egg white in small bowl with electric mixer until soft peaks form; gradually add sifted icing sugar. Fold egg white mixture into cream; fold in fruit and nuts.

**tip**  Cassata can be made a week ahead; keep, covered, in freezer.

**per serving**  34.4g total fat (20.4g saturated fat); 2307kJ (552 cal); 57.8g carbohydrate; 6.6g protein; 0.7g fibre

"My boyfriend's mum has got all her friends making this recipe. It is so yummy; great in the festive season."

Sharon Reeve
is the youngest member of the Test Kitchen. She started as a junior almost two years ago, and is now assistant food editor of *Woman's Day*.

# frozen mocha mousse

PREPARATION TIME 1 HOUR (PLUS FREEZING AND REFRIGERATION TIME) **SERVES** 10

### DARK CHOCOLATE LAYER

100g dark eating chocolate, melted
2 teaspoons coffee-flavoured liqueur
2 eggs, separated
½ cup (125ml) thickened cream

### MILK CHOCOLATE LAYER

100g milk eating chocolate, melted
2 tablespoons coffee-flavoured liqueur
2 eggs, separated
½ cup (125ml) thickened cream

### WHITE CHOCOLATE LAYER

120g white eating chocolate, melted
60g butter, melted
2 teaspoons coffee-flavoured liqueur
3 eggs, separated
⅔ cup (160ml) thickened cream

### NUTTY CHOCOLATE SAUCE

½ cup (165g) hazelnut spread
¾ cup (180ml) thickened cream
1 tablespoon coffee-flavoured liqueur

"This dessert was placed in the freezer to set for tasting. It was forgotten – and the Mocha Mousse became Frozen Mocha Mousse."

Karen Green
worked in several different positions in the Test Kitchen during the late '80s and early '90s, latterly as assistant food editor and finally freelancer.

1 Line 14cm x 21cm loaf pan with plastic wrap.
2 To make dark chocolate layer, combine chocolate, liqueur and egg yolks in large bowl, stir until smooth. Whip cream in small bowl until soft peaks form, fold into chocolate mixture. Beat egg whites in small bowl until soft peaks form, fold into chocolate mixture.
3 Pour dark chocolate mixture into prepared dish; cover with foil, freeze until firm.
4 Top with milk chocolate layer, cover; freeze until firm.
5 Top with white chocolate layer, cover; freeze until firm.
6 Turn mousse onto serving plate; remove plastic wrap. Slice mousse, serve with nutty chocolate sauce.

**milk chocolate layer** Combine chocolate, liqueur and egg yolks in large bowl, stir until smooth. Whip cream in small bowl until soft peaks form, fold into chocolate mixture. Beat egg whites in small bowl until soft peaks form, fold into chocolate mixture.

**white chocolate layer** Combine chocolate, butter, liqueur and egg yolks in large bowl, stir until smooth. Whip cream in small bowl until soft peaks form, fold into chocolate mixture. Beat egg whites in small bowl until soft peaks form, fold into chocolate mixture.

**nutty chocolate sauce** Place hazelnut spread in heatproof bowl, stir over hot water until pourable, gradually stir in cream and liqueur; refrigerate until cool.

**tips** The mousse can be made up to a week ahead; keep, covered, in freezer. Any coffee-flavoured liqueur, such as Kahlua or Tia Maria, can be used.

**per serving** 45.4g total fat (26.2g saturated fat); 2449kJ (586 cal); 34.9g carbohydrate; 9.2g protein; 0.4g fibre

# poached plums with almond milk ice-cream

**PREPARATION TIME** 20 MINUTES

**COOKING TIME** 40 MINUTES (PLUS STANDING, COOLING AND FREEZING TIME) **SERVES** 4

2 cups (500ml) water
½ cup (70g) toasted slivered almonds
1 vanilla bean
300ml cream
¾ cup (165g) caster sugar
6 egg yolks

## POACHED PLUMS
2 cups (500ml) water
1 cup (250ml) port
½ cup (110g) caster sugar
1 cinnamon stick
4 plums (450g), halved, seeded

1 Blend or process the water and nuts until fine. Strain almond milk through a muslin-lined strainer into medium saucepan; discard solids.
2 Halve vanilla bean lengthways, scrape seeds into pan with almond milk. Add pod with cream and ¼ cup of the sugar to pan; bring to a boil. Remove from heat; stand 30 minutes. Discard pod.
3 Line 14cm x 21cm loaf pan with baking paper.
4 Beat egg yolks and remaining sugar in medium bowl with electric mixer until thick and creamy. Gradually stir in almond milk mixture; return to same pan. Cook, stirring, over low heat, without boiling, until mixture thickens slightly. Remove from heat; cool to room temperature. Pour ice-cream mixture into loaf pan, cover with foil; freeze until firm.
5 Remove ice-cream from freezer, turn into large bowl; chop ice-cream coarsely then beat with electric mixer until smooth. Return to loaf pan, cover; freeze until firm.
6 Meanwhile, make poached plums.
7 Slice ice-cream; divide among serving plates. Top with plums and syrup.
   **poached plums** Stir the water, port, sugar and cinnamon in medium saucepan, without boiling, until sugar dissolves. Add plums; cook, uncovered, over low heat, about 30 minutes or until just tender. Remove plums from syrup; discard skins. Bring syrup to a boil; boil, uncovered, about 10 minutes or until syrup is reduced to about 1 cup. Remove from heat, discard cinnamon; cool 10 minutes. Refrigerate, covered, until cold.
   **per serving** 51g total fat (24.9g saturated fat); 3712kJ (888 cal); 86.3g carbohydrate; 10.3g protein; 3.5g fibre

"With the tang of seasonal plums and the subtle flavour of almond ice-cream, this is always a crowd pleaser."

Vanessa Vetter loves making ice-cream, and created this dessert during her Test Kitchen days. She has had a varied career – as a cooking demonstrator, in catering and with a home appliance company.

# hot passionfruit soufflé with raspberry cream

PREPARATION TIME 25 MINUTES  COOKING TIME 10 MINUTES  SERVES 4

1 tablespoon caster sugar

2 eggs, separated

½ cup passionfruit pulp

2 tablespoons lemon juice

¾ cup (120g) icing sugar

4 egg whites

## RASPBERRY CREAM

125g frozen raspberries, thawed

300ml thickened cream

1 tablespoon icing sugar

1 tablespoon orange-flavoured liqueur

1 Make raspberry cream. Refrigerate until required.

2 Preheat oven to hot (220°C/200°C fan-forced). Lightly grease four 1-cup (250ml) soufflé dishes, sprinkle inside each one with caster sugar; shake away excess.

3 Combine yolks, passionfruit, juice and half of the sifted icing sugar in large bowl.

4 Beat all the egg whites in small bowl with electric mixer until soft peaks form; add remaining sifted icing sugar and continue beating until firm peaks form. Gently fold a quarter of the whites into passionfruit mixture, then fold in remaining whites.

5 Place dishes on oven tray. Spoon soufflé mixture into prepared dishes; bake about 10 minutes or until puffed and browned.

6 Dust soufflés with a little extra sifted icing sugar, if desired. Serve immediately with raspberry cream.

raspberry cream  Push thawed raspberries through sieve to remove seeds. Whip cream and icing sugar until soft peaks form, beat in sugar; fold in the raspberry puree and liqueur.

tips  You will need about six passionfruit for this recipe.

Soufflés must be made just before serving.

We used Grand Marnier in this recipe, but you can use any citrus-flavoured liqueur, such as Curacao or Cointreau.

per serving  30.5g total fat (19g saturated fat); 2082kJ (498 cal); 45.6g carbohydrate; 9.9g protein; 6g fibre

"This is the perfect beginner's 'scared-to-make-a-soufflé', foolproof recipe."
Lucy Kelly (nee Clayton) was the first home economist taken on by Pamela Clark as food editor. She worked in the Test Kitchen from 1984 to 1987, left to have children and returned in 1995 to 1997. She now does freelance work.

"My father was an avid gardener, and always had a flourishing passionfruit vine. This soufflé was one his favourites."
Margaret Speechly worked in the Test Kitchen, from 1979 to 1982, then left for Melbourne and began teaching home economics to secondary school students. She's married, has two teenage daughters, and teaches part-time.

# marshmallow pavlova

PREPARATION TIME 25 MINUTES  COOKING TIME 1 HOUR 30 MINUTES (PLUS COOLING TIME)
SERVES 8

4 egg whites
1 cup (220g) caster sugar
½ teaspoon vanilla extract
¾ teaspoon white vinegar
300ml thickened cream, whipped
250g strawberries

1 Preheat oven to very slow (120°C/100°C fan-forced). Line oven tray with foil. Grease foil, dust with cornflour; shake away excess. Mark an 18cm-circle on foil.

2 Beat egg whites in small bowl with electric mixer until soft peaks form; add half of the sugar, beat until dissolved. Gradually add remaining sugar, beating after each addition. When sugar is dissolved, add extract and vinegar, beat until combined.

3 Spread meringue into circle on foil, building up sides to approximately 8cm high.

4 Carefully smooth sides and top of pavlova. Then, with spatula blade, mark decorative grooves round side of pavlova; smooth top again.

5 Bake about 1½ hours; pavlova should be firm to touch. Turn off oven, cool pavlova in oven with door ajar.

6 When pavlova is cold, cut around top edge; the crisp meringue top will fall slightly on top of the marshmallow. Served pavlova topped with cream and strawberries; lightly dust with sifted icing sugar, if desired.

tips  Pavlova can be made a day ahead; keep in an airtight container. Top with cream and strawberries just before serving.

per serving  13.8g total fat (9.1g saturated fat); 1041kJ (249 cal); 29.6g carbohydrate; 3.1g protein; 0.7g fibre

"This was called Peg's Pav (though it was my mum's recipe) and first appeared in the WW in the '70s."

Peggy Frizell spent 1968 to 1978 in the Test Kitchen. Then, for 25 years, she ran her own catering firm Peg's Pantry. A year ago, she started giving cooking classes ("a ton of fun!!"). She has three children, all cooks.

# prune and custard tart

PREPARATION TIME 20 MINUTES (PLUS REFRIGERATION TIME)
COOKING TIME 35 MINUTES (PLUS COOLING TIME) **SERVES** 8

1 ½ cups (250g) seeded prunes
2 tablespoons brandy
300ml cream
3 eggs
⅔ cup (150g) caster sugar
1 teaspoon vanilla extract

PASTRY
1 ¼ cups (185g) plain flour
⅓ cup (55g) icing sugar
¼ cup (30g) almond meal
125g cold butter, chopped
1 egg yolk
1 tablespoon water

"This delicious tart
is such an elegant
dessert, and it's a
favourite because it
is not too rich!"
Jessica Sly
tried work experience with
the Test Kitchen in early 2002.
In mid-year, she was offered
a full-time job working on
*Woman's Day*. She now
styles food, and is the
mother of a daughter.

1 Make pastry; bake tart shell.
2 Reduce oven temperature to slow (150°C/130°C fan-forced).
3 Blend or process prunes and brandy until smooth; spread into cooled tart shell.
4 Bring cream to a boil in small saucepan; remove from heat. Whisk eggs, sugar and extract in small bowl until combined; gradually whisk in hot cream. Pour custard into tart shell; bake, uncovered, about 20 minutes or until custard just sets. Stand 10 minutes; serve tart warm or cold dusted with sifted icing sugar, if desired.

**pastry** Blend or process flour, sugar, almond meal and butter until mixture is crumbly. Add egg yolk and the water; process until ingredients just come together. Enclose in plastic wrap; refrigerate 30 minutes. Grease 26cm-round loose-based flan tin. Roll pastry between sheets of baking paper until large enough to line tin. Lift pastry into tin; press into side, trim edge, prick base all over with fork. Cover; refrigerate 20 minutes. Preheat oven to moderately hot (200°C/180°C fan-forced). Place tin on oven tray; cover pastry with baking paper, fill with dried beans or rice. Bake, uncovered, 10 minutes. Remove paper and beans carefully from tin; bake about 5 minutes or until tart shell browns lightly. Cool to room temperature.

**tip** Tart can be made a day ahead; keep, covered, in refrigerator.

**per serving** 34.3g total fat (20.3g saturated fat); 2383kJ (570 cal); 57.4g carbohydrate; 7.7g protein; 3.7g fibre

# lemon tart

**PREPARATION TIME** 30 MINUTES (PLUS REFRIGERATION TIME)
**COOKING TIME** 55 MINUTES  **SERVES** 8

1¼ cups (185g) plain flour
⅓ cup (55g) icing sugar
¼ cup (30g) almond meal
125g cold butter, chopped
1 egg yolk

### LEMON FILLING

1 tablespoon finely grated lemon rind
½ cup (125ml) lemon juice
5 eggs
¾ cup (165g) caster sugar
1 cup (250ml) thickened cream

"A wedge of this smooth citrus filling with crisp pastry makes a great ending to any meal."

Maria Sampsonis was a home economist in the Test Kitchen, working on more than 20 of the WW cookbooks, before joining *Woman's Day*. She is now the mother of a daughter.

1 Blend or process flour, icing sugar, almond meal and butter until combined. Add egg yolk, process until ingredients just come together. Knead dough on floured surface until smooth. Wrap in plastic wrap, refrigerate 30 minutes.

2 Roll pastry between sheets of baking paper until large enough to line 24cm-round loose-based flan tin. Lift pastry into tin; press into side, trim edge. Cover; refrigerate 30 minutes.

3 Meanwhile, preheat oven to moderately hot (200°C/180°C fan-forced).

4 Place flan tin on oven tray. Line pastry case with baking paper, fill with dried beans or rice. Bake, uncovered, 15 minutes. Remove paper and beans; bake about 10 minutes or until browned lightly.

5 Meanwhile, whisk ingredients for lemon filling in medium bowl; stand 5 minutes.

6 Reduce oven temperature to moderate (180°C/160°C fan-forced).

7 Pour lemon filling into pastry case; bake about 30 minutes or until filling has set slightly, cool.

8 Refrigerate until cold. Serve dusted with sifted icing sugar, if desired.

**tips** You need about three lemons for this tart.

Best made a day ahead; keep, covered, in refrigerator.

**per serving** 30.7g total fat (17.4g saturated fat); 2040kJ (488 cal); 45.9g carbohydrate; 8.6g protein; 1.3g fibre

# black forest cheesecake

**PREPARATION TIME** 40 MINUTES (PLUS REFRIGERATION TIME)
**COOKING TIME** 10 MINUTES (PLUS COOLING TIME)  **SERVES** 8

250g plain chocolate biscuits
125g butter, melted
3 teaspoons gelatine
½ cup (125ml) water
250g packet cream cheese, softened
¾ cup (165g) caster sugar
1 tablespoon lemon juice
300ml thickened cream
425g can pitted black cherries

## TOPPING
1 tablespoon cornflour
1 tablespoon caster sugar
1 tablespoon dark rum

1 Blend or process biscuits until mixture resembles fine breadcrumbs. Add butter; process until combined. Press biscuit mixture evenly over base and side of 20cm springform tin, place on oven tray; refrigerate about 30 minutes or until firm.

2 Meanwhile, sprinkle gelatine over the water in small heatproof jug; stand jug in small saucepan of simmering water. Stir until gelatine dissolves; cool 5 minutes.

3 Beat cream cheese, sugar and juice in small bowl with electric mixer until smooth; transfer to large bowl.

4 Whip cream until soft peaks form, fold into cheese mixture in two batches; fold in gelatine mixture. Drain cherries, reserve ¾ cup syrup for topping.

5 Spoon one-third of cheese mixture into crumb crust, top with half of the cherries, repeat layering, ending with cheese mixture. Refrigerate until just firm.

6 Meanwhile, make topping.

7 Spread topping over cheesecake, swirl gently into cheese mixture. Refrigerate cheesecake overnight.

**topping** Blend cornflour and sugar with reserved cherry syrup in small saucepan. Stir over heat until mixture boils and thickens, stir in rum; cool 10 minutes.

**tip** This recipe can be made a day ahead; keep, covered, in refrigerator.

**per serving** 42.4g total fat (26.6g saturated fat); 2533kJ (606 cal); 50.9g carbohydrate; 6.8g protein; 1g fibre

"I've been making this recipe for years; I love the combination of chocolate, cherries and cream."

Kathy Knudsen (nee Wharton) is a trained chef who worked in the Test Kitchen for six years, three of those as a senior home economist. Now working freelance, Kathy has three small children who keep her extremely busy.

# Mars Bar cheesecake

**PREPARATION TIME** 30 MINUTES (PLUS REFRIGERATION TIME)
**COOKING TIME** 5 MINUTES  **SERVES** 8

250g plain chocolate biscuits
125g butter, melted
2 tablespoons brown sugar
20g butter, extra
300ml thickened cream
50g milk eating chocolate, chopped finely
3 teaspoons gelatine
¼ cup (60ml) water
2 x 250g packets cream cheese, softened
½ cup (110g) caster sugar
3 x 60g Mars Bars, chopped finely

1 Blend or process biscuits until mixture resembles fine breadcrumbs. Add butter; process until just combined. Press biscuit mixture evenly over base and side of 20cm springform tin, place on tray; refrigerate about 30 minutes or until firm.

2 Meanwhile, make butterscotch sauce; combine brown sugar, extra butter and 2 tablespoons of the cream in small saucepan. Stir over low heat, without boiling, until sugar dissolves.

3 Make chocolate sauce; combine chocolate and another 2 tablespoons of the cream in another small saucepan; stir over low heat until chocolate melts.

4 Sprinkle gelatine over the water in small heatproof jug; stand jug in small saucepan of simmering water, stir until gelatine dissolves. Cool 5 minutes.

5 Beat cream cheese and caster sugar in medium bowl with electric mixer until smooth. Beat remaining cream in small bowl with electric mixer until soft peaks form. Stir gelatine mixture into cream cheese mixture with Mars Bars; fold in cream.

6 Pour half of the cream cheese mixture into crumb crust; drizzle half of the butterscotch and chocolate sauces over cream cheese mixture. Pull skewer backwards and forwards through mixture to create marbled effect. Repeat with remaining cream cheese mixture and sauces. Cover cheesecake; refrigerate about 3 hours or until set.

**tip** This recipe can be made a day ahead; keep, covered, in refrigerator.

**per serving** 60.3g total fat (37.9g saturated fat); 3357kJ (803 cal); 58.2g carbohydrate; 10.9g protein; 1g fibre

"Wow, all those yummy recipes. The Mars Bar cheesecake ... delicious!"

Laura O'Brien
was food director Pamela Clark's personal assistant. Now working for a property developer in Dublin, she plans to study journalism.

# chocolate mousse cake
# with coffee anglaise

**PREPARATION TIME** 45 MINUTES

**COOKING TIME** 30 MINUTES (PLUS STANDING, COOLING AND REFRIGERATION TIME)  **SERVES** 10

6 eggs, separated
½ cup (80g) icing sugar
¼ cup (25g) cocoa powder
2 tablespoons cornflour
150g dark eating chocolate, melted
1 tablespoon water
1 litre (4 cups) thickened cream
600g dark eating chocolate, melted, extra

### COFFEE ANGLAISE
3 cups (750ml) milk
1 ½ cups (135g) coffee beans
8 egg yolks
¾ cup (165g) caster sugar

1 Make coffee anglaise.
2 Preheat oven to moderate (180°C/160°C fan-forced). Grease 25cm x 30cm swiss roll pan; cover base and short sides of pan with baking paper, bringing paper 5cm above edges.
3 Beat egg yolks and icing sugar in small bowl with electric mixer until light and creamy. Transfer to large bowl. Fold in sifted cocoa powder and cornflour, then chocolate; stir in the water.
4 Beat egg whites in medium bowl with electric mixer until soft peaks form; fold into chocolate mixture in two batches. Spread mixture into pan; bake about 15 minutes. Turn cake onto wire rack covered with baking paper; cool to room temperature.
5 Cut out circle of cake large enough to fit 26cm springform tin, using smaller pieces to fit, if necessary. Beat cream in large bowl with electric mixer until slightly thickened. Fold in slightly cooled extra melted chocolate in four batches. Pour mixture over cake base, refrigerate until set.
6 Remove cake from tin, dust with a little extra sifted cocoa, if desired; serve with coffee anglaise.

**coffee anglaise** Combine milk and beans in large saucepan, bring to a boil; remove from heat, cover, stand 1 hour. Whisk egg yolks and sugar in large bowl, whisk in milk mixture. Return mixture to same pan, stir over heat, without boiling, until slightly thickened, strain; cool to room temperature. Cover, refrigerate until cold.

**tip** Recipe can be made two days ahead; keep, covered, in refrigerator.

**per serving** 69.2g total fat (41.4g saturated fat); 4126kJ (987 cal); 80.9g carbohydrate; 15.7g protein; 1.3g fibre

"This is a sensational do-ahead special-occasion dessert cake. It keeps really well and is perfect for a large group."

Cynthia Black
came to the Test Kitchen in the early 1990s, and left in 1993, continuing her food career at Darling Mills, her family's restaurant in Sydney. She has now gone into business for herself, selling olives, dips and sauces.

# apple pie

PREPARATION TIME 45 MINUTES (PLUS REFRIGERATION TIME)
COOKING TIME 35 MINUTES (PLUS COOLING TIME) SERVES 8

1½ cups (225g) plain flour
¾ cup (110g) self-raising flour
⅓ cup (50g) cornflour
½ cup (60g) custard powder
185g cold butter, chopped
1 tablespoon white sugar
1 egg, separated
⅓ cup (80ml) iced water, approximately
2 tablespoons apricot jam
2 teaspoons white sugar, extra

## FILLING

7 large green-skinned apples (1.5kg)
½ cup (125ml) water
¼ cup (55g) white sugar
½ teaspoon ground cinnamon
1 teaspoon finely grated lemon rind

1 Make filling.
2 Sift flours and custard powder into large bowl; rub in butter, add sugar. Make well in centre, add egg yolk and enough of the water to mix to a firm dough; knead lightly. Cover; refrigerate 1 hour.
3 Preheat oven to moderately hot (200°C/180°C fan-forced).
4 Roll out just over half of the pastry, on floured surface, until just large enough to line a 23cm pie plate. Lift pastry into pie plate; press into side, trim edge. Spread base of pastry with apricot jam, top with filling.
5 Roll out remaining pastry until large enough to cover pie. Brush edges of pie with a little lightly beaten egg white; cover with pastry. Press edges together firmly, trim and decorate. Brush pastry with egg white; sprinkle with extra sugar. Cut a few slits in pastry to allow steam to escape. Bake about 25 minutes or until golden brown.

**filling** Peel, quarter and core apples; cut each quarter in half lengthways. Combine apples in large saucepan with the water, sugar, cinnamon and rind. Bring to a boil, simmer, covered, about 5 minutes or until apples are almost tender. Remove from heat; drain, cool to room temperature.

**per serving** 20.3g total fat (12.8g saturated fat); 1952kJ (467 cal); 66.2g carbohydrate; 5.9g protein; 4.3g fibre

"This apple pie is the best I have tasted. Crisp and light, it reminds me of grandma's apple pie."

Michelle Noerianto (nee Gorry) discovered a passion for food when she came into the Test Kitchen, aged 14, to work for then food editor Ellen Sinclair. She's now has two children, and works as a freelancer.

# baking

Passion and technique combine to create a masterpiece

# lemon sour cream cake

PREPARATION TIME 35 MINUTES  COOKING TIME 1 HOUR 30 MINUTES (PLUS COOLING TIME)
SERVES 12

250g butter, softened
2 tablespoons grated lemon rind
2 cups (440g) caster sugar
6 eggs
2 cups (300g) plain flour
¼ cup (35g) self-raising flour
¾ cup (180g) sour cream

1 Preheat oven to moderately slow (170°C/150°C fan-forced). Grease deep
  27cm-round cake pan; line base with baking paper.
2 Beat butter, rind and sugar in large bowl with electric mixer until light and
  fluffy; beat in eggs one at a time. Stir in half the sifted flours and half the sour
  cream, then stir in remaining flours and remaining sour cream until smooth.
3 Spread mixture into pan; bake about 1½ hours. Stand cake 5 minutes before
  turning onto wire rack to cool. Dust with sifted icing sugar before serving,
  if desired.
  **tip**  Cake can be made a week ahead; store in an airtight container.
  **per serving**  26g total fat (16g saturated fat); 2015kJ (482 cal); 57.4g carbohydrate;
  6.8g protein; 1.1g fibre

"Easy to make as
it's mixed in just
one bowl, this cake
has a really lemony
flavour, it's moist
and keeps well."

Karen Buckley
still works in the food
industry after almost
20 years and having had
three children. Karen still
finds time to enjoy cooking
and entertaining friends.

# mississippi mud cake

**PREPARATION TIME** 10 MINUTES  **COOKING TIME** 1 HOUR 20 MINUTES (PLUS COOLING TIME)
**SERVES** 9

250g butter, chopped
150g dark eating chocolate, chopped
2 cups (440g) white sugar
1 cup (250ml) hot water
⅓ cup (80ml) whisky
1 tablespoon instant coffee granules
1½ cups (225g) plain flour
¼ cup (35g) self-raising flour
¼ cup (25g) cocoa powder
2 eggs, beaten lightly

1 Preheat oven to moderately slow (170°C/150°C fan-forced). Grease 23cm-square slab pan; line base and sides with baking paper.
2 Combine butter, chocolate, sugar, the water, whisky and coffee in medium saucepan; stir over low heat until mixture is smooth, cool. Stir in sifted flours and cocoa then egg.
3 Pour into pan; bake about 1¼ hours. Stand 10 minutes; turn onto wire rack to cool. Serve dusted with sifted icing sugar, if desired.
   **per serving** 29.4g total fat (18.5g saturated fat); 2583kJ (618 cal); 81g carbohydrate; 6.2g protein; 1.5g fibre

"This cake depicts what food is all about for me... it enlivens my tastebuds and tempts my sweet-tooth."
Karen Lynne Hughes began her career in the Test Kitchen in 1981 and has continued writing for the corporate food industry.

"A chocolate cake can never be too chocolate-y."
Wendy Berecry worked in the Test Kitchen from 1984 to 1988. It was her launch pad to a freelance career in food styling for magazines, books, advertising and television.

# dark chocolate and almond torte

PREPARATION TIME 20 MINUTES  COOKING TIME 55 MINUTES (PLUS COOLING AND STANDING TIME)
SERVES 14

160g dark eating chocolate, chopped coarsely
160g butter, chopped
5 eggs, separated
¾ cup (165g) caster sugar
1 cup (120g) almond meal
⅔ cup (50g) toasted flaked almonds, chopped coarsely
⅓ cup (35g) coarsely grated dark eating chocolate
1 cup (150g) vienna almonds

DARK CHOCOLATE GANACHE
125g dark eating chocolate, chopped coarsely
⅓ cup (80ml) thickened cream

1 Preheat oven to moderate (180°C/160°C fan-forced). Grease deep 22cm-round cake pan; line base and side with baking paper.

2 Stir chopped chocolate and butter in small saucepan over low heat until smooth; cool to room temperature.

3 Beat egg yolks and sugar in small bowl with electric mixer until thick and creamy. Transfer to large bowl; fold in chocolate mixture, almond meal, flaked almonds and grated chocolate.

4 Beat egg whites in small bowl with electric mixer until soft peaks form; fold into chocolate mixture in two batches. Pour mixture into pan; bake about 45 minutes. Stand cake in pan 15 minutes; turn cake, top-side up, onto wire rack to cool.

5 Meanwhile, stir ingredients for dark chocolate ganache in small saucepan over low heat until smooth.

6 Spread ganache over cake, decorate cake with vienna almonds; stand 30 minutes before serving.

tip  Vienna almonds are whole almonds coated in toffee; they are available from selected supermarkets, gourmet food and specialty confectionery stores and nut shops.

per serving  30.2g total fat (12.7g saturated fat); 1735kJ (415 cal); 30.6g carbohydrate; 7.5g protein; 1.9g fibre

"Seriously delicious and not for the faint-hearted, but if you're going to have a cake, you may as well make it a good one."

Sammie Coryton daughter of Sarah Coryton (page 53), was a home economist in the Test Kitchen before being poached to work in TV, as supervising chef on *Fresh with The Australian Women's Weekly*, on the Nine Network.

# white chocolate mud cake

PREPARATION TIME 50 MINUTES  COOKING TIME 1 HOUR 45 MINUTES (PLUS COOLING TIME)
SERVES 12

250g butter, chopped
180g white eating chocolate, chopped coarsely
1 ½ cups (330g) caster sugar
¾ cup (180ml) milk
1 ½ cups (225g) plain flour
½ cup (75g) self-raising flour
½ teaspoon vanilla extract
2 eggs, beaten lightly

## WHITE CHOCOLATE GANACHE
½ cup (125ml) thickened cream
360g white eating chocolate, chopped finely

## CHOCOLATE CURLS
1 ⅓ cups (200g) dark chocolate Melts, melted
1 ⅓ cups (200g) white chocolate Melts, melted
1 ⅓ cups (200g) milk chocolate Melts, melted

1 Preheat oven to moderately slow (170°C/150°C fan-forced). Grease deep
   20cm-round cake pan; line base and side with baking paper.
2 Combine butter, chocolate, sugar and milk in medium saucepan; stir over
   low heat until melted. Transfer mixture to large bowl; cool 15 minutes.
3 Stir in sifted flours, extract and egg; pour into pan. Bake about 1 hour 40 minutes;
   cool cake in pan.
4 Meanwhile, make white chocolate ganache and chocolate curls.
5 Turn cake onto serving plate, top-side up. Spread ganache all over cake; top
   with chocolate curls.
   **white chocolate ganache** Bring cream to a boil in small saucepan, pour over
   chocolate in medium bowl; stir with wooden spoon until chocolate melts. Cover
   bowl; refrigerate, stirring occasionally, about 30 minutes or until spreadable.
   **chocolate curls** Spread dark, white and milk chocolate separately on marble slab
   or bench top. When chocolate is almost set, drag ice-cream scoop over surface of
   chocolate to make curls. Set chocolate can be scraped up, re-melted and used again.
   **per serving** 52.5g total fat (33g saturated fat); 3762kJ (900 cal); 101.1g carbohydrate;
   11.2g protein; 1.3g fibre

"This recipe is a favourite that I make for birthdays and other special family occasions."

Kimberley Coverdale started in the Test Kitchen in 1997 as a junior home economist, became Test Kitchen manager in 2001 then joined *Woman's Day* in 2003 as the deputy food editor, leaving in 2005 to work in the same capacity for another magazine.

"An easy way to fill my biscuit tin for a hungry family! I use it now to teach my grandchildren how to cook."

Helen Halfpenny ran the Test Kitchen between 1967 and 1969, before leaving to have twins (just two weeks later!). She then helped her husband run a family dairy farm and today is director of a milk-processing plant.

# anzac biscuits

**PREPARATION TIME** 30 MINUTES  **COOKING TIME** 25 MINUTES PER TRAY (PLUS COOLING TIME)
**MAKES** 25 BISCUITS

1 cup (90g) rolled oats
1 cup (150g) plain flour
1 cup (220g) caster sugar
¾ cup (60g) desiccated coconut
125g butter, chopped
1 tablespoon golden syrup
1½ teaspoons bicarbonate of soda
2 tablespoons boiling water

1 Preheat oven to slow (150°C/130°C fan-forced). Lightly grease oven trays.

2 Combine oats, flour, sugar and coconut in large bowl.

3 Combine butter and syrup in small saucepan; stir over low heat until smooth.

4 Combine soda and the boiling water in small bowl, add to butter mixture; stir into dry ingredients while warm.

5 Place level tablespoons of mixture onto trays about 5cm apart; press lightly. Bake about 25 minutes. Loosen biscuits on trays while warm; cool on trays.

**tip** Biscuits can be made up to two weeks ahead; store in an airtight container.

**per biscuit** 6g total fat (4.2g saturated fat); 514kJ (123 cal); 16.4g carbohydrate; 1.2g protein; 0.8g fibre

# cinnamon teacake

**PREPARATION TIME** 15 MINUTES  **COOKING TIME** 25 MINUTES **SERVES** 8

60g butter, softened
½ cup (110g) caster sugar
1 egg
1 teaspoon vanilla extract
1 cup (150g) self-raising flour
⅓ cup (80ml) milk
15g butter, melted, extra
1 tablespoon caster sugar, extra
1 teaspoon ground cinnamon

1 Preheat oven to moderate (180°C/160°C fan-forced). Grease deep 20cm-round cake pan; line base with baking paper.
2 Beat butter, sugar, egg and extract until light and creamy; add sifted flour and milk, stir until smooth.
3 Spread mixture into pan; bake 25 minutes. Stand cake in pan 5 minutes before turning onto wire rack; brush top with extra butter, sprinkle with combined extra sugar and cinnamon.

**tip** Cake can be made two days ahead; store in an airtight container.

**per serving** 9g total fat (5.6g saturated fat); 874kJ (209 cal); 29.8g carbohydrate; 3.1g protein; 0.7g fibre

# tiramisu torte

**PREPARATION TIME** 30 MINUTES  **COOKING TIME** 25 MINUTES (PLUS COOLING TIME)  **SERVES** 12

6 eggs
1 cup (220g) caster sugar
½ cup (75g) plain flour
½ cup (75g) self-raising flour
½ cup (75g) cornflour
¼ cup (10g) instant coffee granules
1 ½ cups (375ml) boiling water
¾ cup (180ml) marsala
¼ cup (60ml) coffee-flavoured liqueur
300ml thickened cream
½ cup (80g) icing sugar
3 cups (750g) mascarpone
3⅓ cups (500g) vienna almonds, chopped coarsely

1 Preheat oven to moderate (180°C/160°C fan-forced). Grease two deep 22cm-round cake pans; line bases with baking paper.

2 Beat eggs in medium bowl with electric mixer about 10 minutes or until thick and creamy. Add caster sugar, 1 tablespoon at a time, beating until sugar is dissolved between additions. Gently fold triple-sifted flours into egg mixture. Divide cake mixture evenly between pans; bake about 25 minutes. Turn cakes, top-side up, onto wire racks to cool.

3 Meanwhile, dissolve coffee in the boiling water in small heatproof bowl. Stir in marsala and liqueur; cool.

4 Beat cream and icing sugar in small bowl with electric mixer until soft peaks form; transfer to large bowl. Stir in mascarpone and ½ cup of the coffee mixture.

5 Split cooled cakes in half. Centre half of one cake on serving plate; brush with a quarter of the remaining coffee mixture then spread with about 1 cup of the cream mixture. Repeat layering until last cake half is covered with cream. Spread remaining cream around side of cake; press almonds all over cake. Refrigerate.

**tips** This cake is best made a day ahead; keep, refrigerated, in airtight container. Vienna almonds are whole almonds that have been coated in a toffee mixture. Any coffee-flavoured liqueur, such as Kahlua or Tia Maria, can be used in this recipe.

**per serving** 56.9g total fat (28.3g saturated fat); 3457kJ (827 cal); 62.8g carbohydrate; 13.7g protein; 3.1g fibre

"This is the cake I made when my boyfriend came over to my parents' home to ask for my hand in marriage. Everyone loved it."

Amira Georgy (nee Ibram) has degrees in journalism and Japanese. A food lover, she interviewed Pamela Clark then said, "I want a job here!" After four years as assistant food editor on the Test Kitchen cookbooks, Amira joined the editorial team of a food and lifestyle magazine.

"This recipe was the favourite family celebration cake, so I made it often for birthdays."

Sue Christmas
was a home economist in the Test Kitchen under former food editor Ellen Sinclair, from 1973 to 1979, working on the WW recipe cards – some of which she still uses!

# strawberry hazelnut gateau

PREPARATION TIME 1 HOUR  COOKING TIME 35 MINUTES (PLUS COOLING AND REFRIGERATION TIME)
SERVES 8

4 egg whites
1¼ cups (275g) caster sugar
1 cup (100g) hazelnut meal
1 teaspoon white vinegar
½ teaspoon vanilla extract
185g dark eating chocolate, melted
20g butter, melted
1¾ cup (430ml) thickened cream, whipped
125g strawberries, halved

1 Preheat oven to moderate (180°C/160°C fan-forced). Grease two 20cm springform tins; line base and sides with baking paper, grease paper, sprinkle with cornflour, shake away excess.

2 Beat egg whites in small bowl with electric mixer until soft peaks form; gradually add sugar, beating until sugar is dissolved between each addition. Fold in hazelnut meal, vinegar and extract.

3 Spread meringue mixture evenly into tins; bake about 35 minutes or until meringue is crisp. Release sides of tins; cool meringues on base of tins.

4 Combine chocolate and butter in small bowl.

5 Remove meringue layers from bases. Place one layer on plate, flat-side down; spread with half of the chocolate mixture, top with half of the cream and the strawberries.

6 Spread flat side of second meringue layer with remaining chocolate mixture, place on top of strawberry layer, chocolate-side down. Cover top of cake with remaining cream. Refrigerate 3 hours or overnight. Dust with sifted cocoa powder before serving, if desired.

tips Meringue layers can be made three days ahead; store in airtight container.
Gateau is best assembled the day before; keep, covered, in refrigerator.
For a really decedent dessert, the gateau can be completely covered in whipped cream. This also helps soften the meringue, making it easier to cut.
per serving 36.1g total fat (18.6g saturated fat); 2270kJ (543 cal); 51.7g carbohydrate; 6.2g protein; 1.9g fibre

# greek yogurt cake

**PREPARATION TIME** 25 MINUTES  **COOKING TIME** 35 MINUTES (PLUS COOLING TIME)  **SERVES** 12

125g butter, softened
1 cup (220g) caster sugar
3 eggs, separated
2 cups (300g) self-raising flour
½ teaspoon bicarbonate soda
¼ cup (40g) finely chopped blanched almonds
1 cup (280g) yogurt

1 Preheat oven to moderate (180°C/160°C fan-forced). Lightly grease 20cm x 30cm lamington pan; line base and sides with baking paper.

2 Beat butter and sugar in small bowl with electric mixer until light and fluffy. Add egg yolks, beat well.

3 Transfer mixture to large bowl; stir in sifted flour and soda in two batches, then nuts and yogurt.

4 Beat egg whites in small bowl with electric mixer until soft peaks form. Gently fold egg whites into yogurt mixture in two batches. Spread mixture into pan. Bake about 35 minutes. Turn cake onto wire rack to cool; dust with sifted icing sugar, if desired.

**per serving**  12.8g total fat (6.7g saturated fat); 1216kJ (291 cal); 37.3g carbohydrate; 5.9g protein; 1.2g fibre

"A gorgeous cake, simple to make, great to eat on its own or with cream and poached quinces."

Kathy Snowball was an assistant food editor in the Test Kitchen before joining *Australian Gourmet Traveller* as food editor. These days, Kathy is part owner of a handmade biscuits and cakes business and a freelance food writer.

# triple choc brownies

**PREPARATION TIME** 20 MINUTES  **COOKING TIME** 35 MINUTES (PLUS COOLING TIME)  **SERVES** 12

125g butter, chopped
200g dark eating chocolate, chopped coarsely
½ cup (110g) caster sugar
2 eggs, beaten lightly
1¼ cups (185g) plain flour
150g white eating chocolate, chopped coarsely
100g milk eating chocolate, chopped coarsely

1 Preheat oven to moderate (180°C/160°C fan-forced). Grease deep 19cm-square cake pan; line base and sides with baking paper.

2 Combine butter and dark chocolate in medium saucepan; stir over low heat until melted. Cool 10 minutes.

3 Stir in sugar and egg, then flour; stir in white and milk chocolates. Spread mixture into pan.

4 Bake about 35 minutes or until mixture is firm to touch. Cool in pan. If desired, sprinkle with sifted icing sugar before cutting.

**tip** Brownies can be made three days ahead; store in an airtight container.

**per piece** 20.8g total fat (12.8g saturated fat); 1555kJ (372 cal); 42.8g carbohydrate; 5.3g protein; 0.9g fibre

"This is an absolutely decadent slice that always satisfies the chocolate craving."

Emma Braz
worked in the Test Kitchen from 1995 to 2001, first as a junior, then a home economist and finally training new staff. Today, she has a business selling gluten-free foods.

# Cherry Ripe mud cake

**PREPARATION TIME** 35 MINUTES  **COOKING TIME** 2 HOURS (PLUS COOLING TIME)  **SERVES** 12

"This was made for my 25th birthday by the Test Kitchen team … I love the use of the Cherry Ripe … delicious."

Benjamin Haslam started in the Test Kitchen in 2003, the only male in the place. He helped on the WW cookbooks and *Woman's Day* and is now chef in the ACP Magazines' dining room.

250g butter, chopped
1 tablespoon instant coffee granules
1⅔ cups (400ml) coconut milk
200g dark eating chocolate, chopped coarsely
2 cups (440g) caster sugar
¾ cup (110g) self-raising flour
1 cup (150g) plain flour
¼ cup (25g) cocoa powder
2 eggs, beaten lightly
1 teaspoon vanilla extract
2 x 85g Cherry Ripe bars, chopped coarsely
200g dark eating chocolate, chopped coarsely, extra
125g butter, chopped, extra

## CHOCOLATE PANELS
300g dark chocolate Melts
1 teaspoon vegetable oil

1 Preheat oven to slow (150°C/130°C fan-forced). Grease deep 22cm-round cake pan; line base and side with baking paper.

2 Melt butter in large saucepan; add coffee, coconut milk, chocolate and sugar. Stir over heat until chocolate melts and sugar dissolves; cool to room temperature.

3 Whisk in sifted dry ingredients, then egg and extract; stir in half of the Cherry Ripe. Pour mixture into pan, top with remaining Cherry Ripe; bake about 1¾ hours. Stand cake 10 minutes; turn, top-side up, onto wire rack to cool.

4 Combine extra chocolate and extra butter in small saucepan; stir over low heat until smooth. Refrigerate until mixture is spreadable.

5 Meanwhile, make chocolate panels.

6 Spread chocolate mixture all over cake; place chocolate panels around side of cake. Serve with whipped cream, if desired.

**chocolate panels** Combine chocolate and oil in medium heatproof bowl; stir over medium saucepan of simmering water until smooth. Cut two 6cm x 50cm strips of baking paper. Spread chocolate evenly over strips; lift strips to allow chocolate to drip off paper. Allow chocolate to set, then, using ruler as a guide, cut chocolate into 4cm panels with sharp knife. Carefully peel away baking paper.

**tip** You can also melt the chocolate for the chocolate panels in a microwave oven; melt on MEDIUM (55%) about 1 minute, stirring twice during cooking. Stir in the oil once the chocolate has melted.

**per serving** 54.1g total fat (35.8g saturated fat); 3724kJ (891 cal); 98.1g carbohydrate; 8.2g protein; 2.9g fibre

# perfect honey roll

PREPARATION TIME 20 MINUTES  COOKING TIME 15 MINUTES (PLUS COOLING TIME)  SERVES 8

1 egg, separated
3 egg whites
2 tablespoons treacle
½ cup (175g) golden syrup
½ cup (75g) cornflour
⅓ cup (50g) self-raising flour
1 teaspoon ground ginger
1 teaspoon ground cinnamon
½ teaspoon ground nutmeg
¼ teaspoon ground clove
2 tablespoons boiling water
½ teaspoon bicarbonate of soda
⅓ cup (25g) desiccated coconut

## MOCK CREAM

½ cup (110g) caster sugar
½ teaspoon gelatine
1 tablespoon milk
⅓ cup (80ml) water
125g butter, softened
½ teaspoon vanilla extract

"I lost track of how many times I made this. I was a victim of the 'swiss roll curse' of cracking … It took about three weeks to get it right."

Quinton Kholer worked in the Test Kitchen on eight cookbooks and the menu planners, and styled for *Woman's Day*. Since 1991, he has taught Commercial Cookery at TAFE, and now develops course material.

1 Preheat oven to hot (220°C/200°C fan-forced). Grease 25cm x 30cm swiss roll pan; line base and short sides with baking paper, bringing paper 5cm over edges. Grease the baking paper.

2 Beat the four egg whites in small bowl with electric mixer until soft peaks form. With motor operating, gradually add combined treacle and syrup in a thin stream.

3 Add yolk; beat until mixture is pale and thick. Transfer mixture to large bowl. Fold in triple-sifted flours and spices, and combined water and soda. Pour mixture into pan; gently spreading evenly into corners. Bake about 15 minutes.

4 Meanwhile, make mock cream.

5 Place a piece of baking paper cut the same size as swiss roll pan on bench; sprinkle evenly with coconut. Turn cake onto paper; peel lining paper away. Working quickly, use serrated knife to cut away crisp edges from all sides of roll.

6 Carefully roll cake loosely from one short side by lifting paper and using it to guide roll into shape; stand 10 seconds then unroll. Re-roll cake; cool to room temperature.

7 Gently unroll cake, spread with mock cream, carefully re-roll cake.

**mock cream** Combine sugar, gelatine, milk and water in small saucepan; stir over low heat, without boiling, until sugar and gelatine dissolve. Cool to room temperature. Beat butter and extract in small bowl with electric mixer until as white as possible. With motor operating, gradually beat in milk mixture until fluffy; this will take up to 15 minutes. Mock cream thickens on standing.

**per serving** 17.4g total fat (11.3g saturated fat); 1513kJ (362 cal); 48.3g carbohydrate; 5.2g protein; 0.9g fibre

"Easy to make, they look elegant, and are great for morning or afternoon tea."

Angela Bresnahan worked in the Test Kitchen from 1992 to 1994, after which she moved on to Queensland's Whitsunday Islands, then overseas for five years. She owned and ran a cafe and restaurant, and is now a head chef.

# almond crisps

**PREPARATION TIME** 25 MINUTES  **COOKING TIME** 10 MINUTES PER TRAY (PLUS COOLING TIME)
**MAKES** 15

125g butter, chopped
¼ cup (55g) caster sugar
1 cup (150g) self-raising flour
¼ cup (30g) almond meal
2 tablespoons flaked almonds

1 Preheat oven to moderately hot (200°C/180°C fan-forced). Lightly grease oven trays.
2 Beat butter and sugar in small bowl with electric mixer until smooth. Stir in flour and almond meal.
3 Roll level tablespoons of mixture into balls; place onto trays about 5cm apart. Flatten slightly with a floured fork to 1cm thick; sprinkle with flaked almonds.
4 Bake about 10 minutes or until browned. Stand crisps on trays 5 minutes; transfer to wire racks to cool.
**tip** Crisps can be made up to two weeks ahead; store in an airtight container.
**per biscuit**  9.1g total fat (4.7g saturated fat); 548kJ (131 cal); 10.9g carbohydrate; 1.8g protein; 0.7g fibre

# caramel and chocolate slice

**PREPARATION TIME** 20 MINUTES  **COOKING TIME** 25 MINUTES (PLUS COOLING TIME)  **MAKES** 15

½ cup (75g) plain flour
½ cup (75g) self-raising flour
1 cup (90g) rolled oats
¾ cup (165g) firmly packed brown sugar
150g butter, melted
125g dark eating chocolate, chopped coarsely
½ cup (55g) coarsely chopped walnuts
¼ cup (35g) plain flour, extra
½ cup (125ml) caramel topping

1 Preheat oven to moderate (180°C/160°C fan-forced). Grease 19cm x 29cm rectangular slice pan; line base and two long sides with baking paper, extending paper 2cm above edges.
2 Combine flours, oats and sugar in medium bowl, stir in butter. Press half the mixture into pan. Bake 10 minutes. Remove from oven, sprinkle with chocolate and walnuts.
3 Blend extra flour with caramel topping in small bowl. Drizzle evenly over chocolate and walnuts, then sprinkle with remaining oat mixture.
4 Bake further 15 minutes. Cool in pan; cut into squares before serving.
   **tips** We used a thick, caramel-flavoured ice-cream topping in this recipe.
   **per piece** 14.5g total fat (7.4g saturated fat); 1145kJ (274 cal); 34.1g carbohydrate; 3g protein; 1.3g fibre

# chewy choc-chunk cookies

**PREPARATION TIME** 25 MINUTES (PLUS REFRIGERATION TIME)
**COOKING TIME** 10 MINUTES PER TRAY (PLUS COOLING TIME)  **MAKES** 20

2 eggs
1⅓ cups (295g) firmly packed brown sugar
1 teaspoon vanilla extract
1 cup (150g) plain flour
¾ cup (110g) self-raising flour
½ teaspoon bicarbonate of soda
½ cup (125ml) vegetable oil
1 cup (120g) coarsely chopped toasted pecans
¾ cup (120g) coarsely chopped raisins
1 cup (150g) dark chocolate Melts, halved
½ cup (95g) white Choc Bits

1 Preheat oven to moderately hot (200°C/180°C fan-forced). Grease oven trays.
2 Beat eggs, sugar and extract in small bowl with electric mixer about 1 minute or until mixture becomes lighter in colour.
3 Stir in sifted dry ingredients then remaining ingredients (the mixture will be soft). Cover bowl; refrigerate 1 hour.
4 Roll heaped tablespoons of the mixture into balls; place onto trays about 6cm apart, flatten into 6cm rounds.
5 Bake about 10 minutes or until browned lightly. Stand cookies on trays 5 minutes; transfer to wire rack to cool.

**tips** Cookies can be made up to one week ahead; keep in an airtight container. Walnuts can be substituted for pecans, if desired.

**per cookie** 14.5g total fat (3.5g saturated fat); 1170kJ (280 cal); 35.4g carbohydrate; 3.5g protein; 1.4g fibre

"I make these cookies to have when friends drop in – I'm forever being asked for the recipe."

Kimberley Coverdale started in the Test Kitchen in 1997 as a junior home economist, became Test Kitchen manager in 2001 then joined *Woman's Day* in 2003 as the deputy food editor, leaving in 2005 to work in the same capacity for another magazine.

# moist orange cake

PREPARATION TIME 25 MINUTES  COOKING TIME 45 MINUTES (PLUS COOLING TIME)  SERVES 8

155g butter, softened
2 teaspoons finely grated orange rind
⅔ cup (150g) caster sugar
3 eggs
1¼ cups (185g) self-raising flour
¼ cup (60ml) milk
1 tablespoon desiccated coconut

### ORANGE ICING

1 cup (160g) icing sugar
1 teaspoon butter, softened
1 tablespoon orange juice, approximately

1 Preheat oven to moderate (180°C/160°C fan-forced). Grease deep 20cm-round
   cake pan; line base with baking paper.
2 Combine butter, rind, sugar, eggs, sifted flour and milk in large bowl; beat on
   low speed with electric mixer until combined. Increase speed to medium, beat
   about 3 minutes or until mixture is lighter in colour and smooth.
3 Spread mixture into pan; bake about 45 minutes. Stand cake in pan 5 minutes
   before turning onto wire rack to cool.
4 Meanwhile, make orange icing.
5 Spread cold cake with orange icing; sprinkle with coconut.
   **orange icing** Sift icing sugar into small heatproof bowl, stir in butter and enough
   juice to make a stiff paste. Stir over hot water until icing is spreadable.
   **tip** Can be made two days ahead; keep in an airtight container.
   **per serving** 18.9g total fat (11.7g saturated fat); 1693kJ (405 cal); 55.8g carbohydrate;
   5.2g protein; 1g fibre

"This favourite is
reminiscent of my
mother's New Year's
Eve celebration cake;
simple, flavoursome
and economical."
Voula Mantzouridis
spent just over a year in
the Test Kitchen; she is now
a freelance food consultant.

# nanaimo bars

**PREPARATION TIME** 45 MINUTES (PLUS REFRIGERATION TIME)  **MAKES** 16

185g butter, chopped
100g dark eating chocolate, coarsely chopped
1 egg
2 cups (200g) wheatmeal biscuit crumbs
1 cup (80g) desiccated coconut
⅔ cup (80g) finely chopped pecans

## FILLING
60g butter, softened
1 teaspoon vanilla extract
2 cups (320g) icing sugar
2 tablespoons custard powder
¼ cup (60ml) milk

## TOPPING
30g dark eating chocolate
15g butter

1 Grease 19cm x 29cm rectangular slice pan; line base and two long sides with baking paper, extending paper 2cm above edges.
2 Make filling.
3 Melt butter and chocolate in large bowl over hot water until smooth; stir in egg.
4 Add biscuit crumbs, coconut and nuts; mix well. Press mixture firmly over base of pan. Spread evenly with filling. Refrigerate until firm.
5 Make topping.
6 Drizzle slice with topping; refrigerate 3 hours or overnight until set. Cut into pieces before serving.

**filling** Beat butter and extract in small bowl with electric mixer until as white as possible; gradually beat in sifted icing sugar and custard powder, then milk.

**topping** Melt chocolate and butter in small bowl over hot water.

**tip** Nanaimo bars can be made up to two weeks ahead; keep, covered, in refrigerator.

The butter and chocolate for the base and topping can be melted together in a microwave oven.

**per piece** 24.9g total fat (14.4g saturated fat); 1526kJ (365 cal); 346g carbohydrate; 2.7g protein; 1.9g fibre

"This was hugely popular in Canada, where it originated, and here, when we published it in the 1980s. It cuts and keeps well."

Laura Robertson was one of the team in the Test Kitchen for two years in the early '80s, before marrying and moving to Canberra, then Perth, where she taught home economics.

"This is my mum's recipe, and whenever I go home, I'll always find one waiting in the cake tin."

Cathie Lonnie worked as a chef in northeast Victoria before becoming a food technologist. Three years ago, she moved to Sydney as a home economist in the Test Kitchen; she is now Test Kitchen manager.

# wendy's sponge cake

PREPARATION TIME 20 MINUTES  COOKING TIME 20 MINUTES (PLUS COOLING TIME)  SERVES 10

4 eggs
¾ cup (165g) caster sugar
⅔ cup (100g) wheaten cornflour
¼ cup (30g) custard powder
1 teaspoon cream of tartar
½ teaspoon bicarbonate of soda
300ml thickened cream
1 tablespoon icing sugar
½ teaspoon vanilla extract
¼ cup (80g) strawberry jam, warmed
250g strawberries, sliced thinly
1 tablespoon icing sugar, extra

1 Preheat oven to moderate (180°C/160°C fan-forced). Grease two deep 22cm-round cake pans; sprinkle with flour, shake away excess.

2 Beat eggs and caster sugar in small bowl with electric mixer about 5 minutes or until thick and creamy; transfer to large bowl.

3 Sift dry ingredients twice onto baking paper before sifting over egg mixture; gently fold ingredients together.

4 Divide mixture evenly between pans; bake about 20 minutes. Turn sponges immediately onto baking-paper-lined wire rack; turn top-side up to cool.

5 Beat cream, icing sugar and extract in small bowl with electric mixer until firm peaks form. Place one cold sponge on serving plate; spread first with jam, then with cream mixture. Top with strawberry slices, then with remaining sponge. Dust with sifted extra icing sugar.

tip When folding flour into egg mixture, you can use a large metal spoon, a rubber spatula, a whisk or use one hand like a rake.

per serving 13.2g total fat (7.9g saturated fat); 1162kJ (278 cal); 37.2g carbohydrate; 3.8g protein; 0.7g fibre

# fudgy-wudgy chocolate cookies

PREPARATION TIME 15 MINUTES  COOKING TIME 10 MINUTES (PLUS COOLING TIME)
MAKES 24

125g butter, chopped
1 teaspoon vanilla extract
1¼ cups (275g) firmly packed brown sugar
1 egg
1 cup (150g) plain flour
¼ cup (35g) self-raising flour
1 teaspoon bicarbonate of soda
⅓ cup (35g) cocoa powder
½ cup (75g) raisins
¾ cup (110g) macadamia nuts, toasted, chopped coarsely
½ cup (95g) dark Choc Bits
½ cup (75g) dark chocolate Melts, halved

1 Preheat oven to moderate (180°C/160°C fan-forced). Line three oven trays
   with baking paper.
2 Beat butter, extract, sugar and egg in medium bowl with electric mixer
   until smooth. Stir in sifted flours, soda and cocoa powder; stir in raisins,
   nuts and both chocolates.
3 Drop rounded tablespoons of mixture onto trays about 4cm apart; press
   each with hand to flatten slightly.
4 Bake 10 minutes. Stand cookies on trays 5 minutes; transfer to wire rack to cool.
   **tips** Cookies can be made up to one week ahead; store in an airtight container.
   Other nuts, such as walnuts or pecans, can be used instead of macadamias.
   **per cookie** 10.3g total fat (4.7g saturated fat); 807kJ (193 cal); 23.9g carbohydrate;
   2.2g protein; 0.9g fibre

"I made these at home for the family and everyone loved them... one of my favourite cookies."

Elizabeth Macri,
a senior home economist, has been in the Test Kitchen for two years, developing and testing recipes, cooking for photography and helping the Test Kitchen manager.

"I love to make bread; this simple recipe is one I fall back on when I want to have something special."

Sophia Young
is a New York-trained chef who began in the Test Kitchen in 1993. She became an in-house food stylist, but was lured away to *Australian Gourmet Traveller* as associate food editor, staying there until early 2005. She is now food editor of a food and lifestyle magazine.

# olive bread

PREPARATION TIME 45 MINUTES (PLUS STANDING TIME)  COOKING TIME 1 HOUR  SERVES 12

2 teaspoons (7g) dried yeast
1 teaspoon caster sugar
1¼ cups (310ml) warm milk
3⅓ cups (500g) plain flour
1 teaspoon salt
¼ cup (60ml) extra-virgin olive oil
1 cup (120g) seeded black olives, chopped finely

1 Combine yeast, sugar and milk in small jug; stand in warm place about 15 minutes or until mixture is frothy.

2 Sift flour and salt into large bowl. Stir in yeast mixture and oil; mix to a firm dough. Knead dough on floured surface about 5 minutes or until smooth and elastic. Place dough in oiled bowl; cover, stand in warm place about 1½ hours or until dough has doubled in size.

3 Turn dough onto lightly floured surface; knead until smooth. Press dough into 23cm x 28cm rectangle. Spread olives over dough, leaving 2cm border. Roll up dough from long side, tuck ends underneath; place on lightly greased oven tray.

4 Sift a little extra flour over bread. Using scissors, make cuts about 2.5cm apart, along centre of bread. Place bread in warm place; stand, uncovered, about 1 hour or until doubled in size.

5 Meanwhile, preheat oven to moderate (180°C/160°C fan-forced).

6 Bake about 1 hour or until bread is browned and sounds hollow when tapped.

**tip** Bread is best made on day of serving.

**per serving** 6.2g total fat (1.4g saturated fat); 899kJ (215 cal); 33.9g carbohydrate; 5.7g protein; 1.8g fibre

# lime syrup buttermilk cake

PREPARATION TIME 30 MINUTES  COOKING TIME 1 HOUR  SERVES 8

250g butter, softened
1 tablespoon finely grated lime rind
1 cup (220g) caster sugar
3 eggs, separated
2 cups (300g) self-raising flour
1 cup (250ml) buttermilk

**LIME SYRUP**
⅓ cup (80ml) lime juice
¾ cup (165g) caster sugar
¼ cup (60ml) water

1 Preheat oven to moderate (180°C/160°C fan-forced). Grease 20cm baba cake pan; sprinkle with flour, shake away excess.

2 Beat butter, rind and sugar in small bowl with electric mixer until light and fluffy; beat in egg yolks, one at a time, until combined.

3 Transfer mixture to large bowl, stir in half the sifted flour and half the buttermilk, then stir in remaining flour and remaining buttermilk, stir until smooth.

4 Beat egg whites in small bowl with electric mixer until soft peaks form; fold into mixture in two batches.

5 Spread mixture into pan; bake about 1 hour. Stand cake in pan 5 minutes before turning onto serving plate.

6 Meanwhile, combine ingredients for lime syrup in small saucepan, stir over heat until sugar is dissolved, bring to a boil; remove from heat.

7 Gradually pour hot lime syrup evenly over hot cake. Serve cake sprinkled with thinly sliced lime rind, if desired.

**tips** Buttermilk makes a deliciously light cake; if unavailable, use yogurt instead. Lime rind and juice give this cake a fresh flavour, but any citrus rind and juice of your choice can be used.

This cake can also be baked in a deep 20cm-round cake pan. The cake will take about 1½ hours to bake.

Cake can be made two days ahead; keep, covered, in refrigerator.

**per serving** 28.7g total fat (18g saturated fat); 2454kJ (587 cal); 76.7g carbohydrate; 7.8g protein; 1.5g fibre

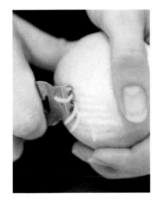

"Beautiful to have with morning or afternoon tea; the zesty, lime-flavoured cake, drenched in warm syrup, makes this a favourite."

Leisel Rogers
was a Test Kitchen member from 1991 to 1994. Moving to Brisbane, she began teaching cooking at a school and in TAFE colleges.

# vanilla currant cookies

PREPARATION TIME 45 MINUTES   COOKING TIME 10 MINUTES PER TRAY (PLUS COOLING TIME)

MAKES 40

125g butter, softened

1 teaspoon vanilla extract

¾ cup (165g) caster sugar

1 egg

2 cups (300g) self-raising flour

½ cup (40g) desiccated coconut

¼ cup (40g) dried currants

## VANILLA ICING

1½ cups (240g) icing sugar

2 teaspoons vanilla extract

1½ teaspoons butter, softened

1 tablespoon milk, approximately

1 Preheat oven to moderately hot (200°C/180°C fan-forced). Grease oven trays.

2 Beat butter, extract, sugar and egg in small bowl with electric mixer until light and fluffy. Transfer mixture to large bowl, stir in sifted flour, coconut and currants.

3 Shape rounded teaspoons of mixture into balls; place onto trays about 5cm apart. Flatten with hand until about 5mm thick.

4 Bake about 10 minutes or until browned lightly. Cool on trays.

5 Spread cookies thinly with vanilla icing, place on wire racks to set.

vanilla icing Sift icing sugar into medium heatproof bowl, stir in extract and butter, then enough milk to give a thick paste. Stir over hot water until spreadable.

tip Cookies can be made up to two weeks ahead; store in an airtight container.

per cookie 3.6g total fat (2.4g saturated fat); 414kJ (99 cal); 16.2g carbohydrate; 1g protein; 0.5g fibre

"These cookies are so popular at my place. I love the addition of coconut."
Michelle Noerianto (nee Gorry) discovered a passion for food when she came into the Test Kitchen, aged 14, to work for then food editor Ellen Sinclair. These days she works as a freelancer.

# apricot chocolate chip cake

**PREPARATION TIME** 30 MINUTES (PLUS STANDING TIME)
**COOKING TIME** 1 HOUR 15 MINUTES (PLUS COOKING TIME) **SERVES** 8

1 cup (150g) chopped dried apricots
1 cup (250ml) apricot nectar
125g butter, softened
⅔ cup (150g) raw sugar
2 eggs, separated
1½ cups (120g) desiccated coconut
1½ cups (225g) self-raising flour
½ cup (95g) dark Choc Bits

1 Preheat oven to moderate (180°C/160°C fan-forced). Grease deep 20cm-round cake pan; line base with baking paper.
2 Combine apricots and nectar in medium bowl; stand 1 hour.
3 Beat butter and sugar in small bowl with electric mixer until light and fluffy. Add egg yolks, beat until combined.
4 Transfer mixture to large bowl, stir in coconut then half the sifted flour and half the apricot mixture. Stir in remaining flour, remaining apricot mixture then Choc Bits.
5 Beat egg whites in small bowl with electric mixer until soft peaks form; fold into apricot mixture.
6 Spread mixture into pan; bake about 1¼ hours. Stand cake 5 minutes before turning onto wire rack to cool.
7 Serve cake dusted with sifted icing sugar, if desired.
**tip** Cake will keep in an airtight container for up to three days.
**per serving** 27.7g total fat (19.5g saturated fat); 2119kJ (507 cal); 59.7g carbohydrate; 7g protein; 5.1g fibre

"This cake has been made dozens of times for birthdays; it's delicious and moist, and keeps well."

Anne Kelly
worked as an editorial assistant in the Test Kitchen in the late '70s. She now lives in Adelaide, works part-time in the food business and is the mother of 3 children.

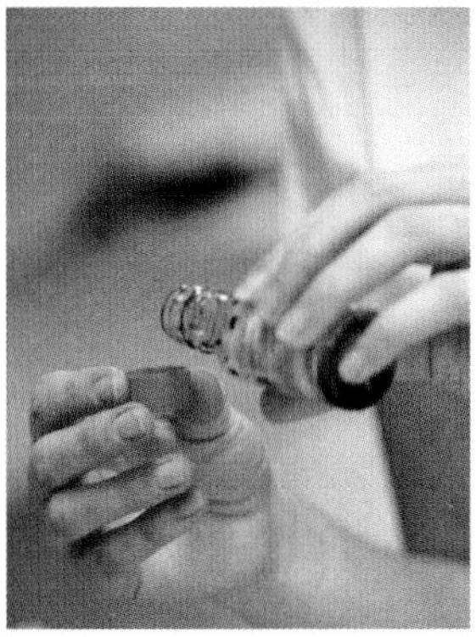

"Jon Allen was the first male employed in the Test Kitchen. He was a gifted cook, and many of his recipes remain favourites, in particular, this one. Thank you from all of us, Jonnie."

Pamela Clark, in memory of Jon Allen.

# moist coconut cake
# with coconut ice frosting

**PREPARATION TIME** 25 MINUTES  **COOKING TIME** 1 HOUR (PLUS COOLING TIME)  **SERVES** 10

125g butter, softened
½ teaspoon coconut essence
1 cup (220g) caster sugar
2 eggs
½ cup (40g) desiccated coconut
1½ cups (225g) self-raising flour
300g sour cream
⅓ cup (80ml) milk

## COCONUT ICE FROSTING

2 cups (320g) icing sugar
1⅓ cups (110g) desiccated coconut
2 egg whites, beaten lightly
pink food colouring

1 Preheat oven to moderate (180°C/160°C fan-forced). Grease deep 22cm-round cake pan; line base with baking paper.
2 Beat butter, essence and sugar in small bowl with electric mixer until light and fluffy. Beat in eggs, one at a time.
3 Transfer mixture to large bowl. Stir in half the coconut and half the sifted flour, half the sour cream and half the milk, then add remaining coconut, flour, sour cream and milk; stir until smooth.
4 Spread mixture into pan; bake about 1 hour. Stand cake in pan 5 minutes before turning onto wire rack to cool.
5 Meanwhile, make coconut ice frosting.
6 Top cold cake with coconut ice frosting.
   **coconut ice frosting**  Combine sifted icing sugar in bowl with coconut and egg whites; mix well. Tint pink with a little colouring.
   **per serving**  33.6g total fat (23.8g saturated fat); 2516kJ (602 cal); 72.1g carbohydrate; 6.2g protein; 3.1g fibre

# sweet coconut slice

PREPARATION TIME 40 MINUTES (PLUS REFRIGERATION TIME)
COOKING TIME 40 MINUTES (PLUS COOLING TIME)  MAKES 20

"A hit with every coconut lover, this slice just improves with age. It can also be made as tartlets."

Barbara Northwood spent a number of years working in the Test Kitchen, before joining the WW team as deputy food editor. In 1989, she became the food editor of *Woman's Day* magazine, leaving in 2005 to take another editorial position.

1 cup (150g) plain flour
½ cup (75g) self-raising flour
2 tablespoons caster sugar
125g cold butter, chopped
1 egg
1 tablespoon iced water
½ cup (160g) apricot jam
10 red glacé cherries, halved

### COCONUT FILLING

1 cup (250ml) water
1 cup (220g) caster sugar
3½ cups (280g) desiccated coconut
3 eggs, beaten lightly
60g butter, melted
¼ cup (60ml) milk
1 teaspoon vanilla extract
1 teaspoon baking powder

1 Blend or process flours, sugar and butter until combined. Add egg and the water, process until mixture forms a ball; cover, refrigerate 30 minutes.

2 Meanwhile, make coconut filling.

3 Preheat oven to moderate (180°C/160°C fan-forced). Line 25cm x 30cm swiss roll pan with baking paper, extending paper 5cm over long sides.

4 Roll pastry between sheets of baking paper until 3mm thick and large enough to cover base of pan. Gently ease into base of pan.

5 Brush jam evenly over pastry base. Spread coconut mixture over jam.

6 Place cherry halves evenly over slice top. Bake about 35 minutes. Cool in pan; cut into squares before serving.

coconut filling  Combine the water and sugar in small saucepan, stir over heat until sugar is dissolved. Bring to a boil, boil 3 minutes without stirring; cool sugar syrup 5 minutes. Place coconut in large bowl, stir in sugar syrup, egg, butter, milk, extract and baking powder.

tips  Store slice in airtight container for up to four days.
Cooked slice is suitable to freeze, covered, for up to two weeks. Thaw at room temperature.

per tartlet  18g total fat (13.5g saturated fat); 1183kJ (283 cal); 28g carbohydrate; 3.6g protein; 2.6g fibre

# flourless hazelnut chocolate cake

**PREPARATION TIME** 20 MINUTES  **COOKING TIME** 1 HOUR (PLUS STANDING AND COOLING TIME)
**SERVES** 9

Hazelnut meal replaces the flour in this recipe.

⅓ cup (35g) cocoa powder
⅓ cup (80ml) hot water
150g dark eating chocolate, melted
150g butter, melted
1⅓ cups (295g) firmly packed brown sugar
1 cup (100g) hazelnut meal
4 eggs, separated
1 tablespoon cocoa powder, extra

1 Preheat oven to moderate (180°C/160°C fan-forced). Grease deep 19cm-square cake pan; line base and sides with baking paper.
2 Blend cocoa with the hot water in large bowl until smooth. Stir in chocolate, butter, sugar, hazelnut meal and egg yolks.
3 Beat egg whites in small bowl with electric mixer until soft peaks form; fold into chocolate mixture in two batches.
4 Pour mixture into pan; bake about 1 hour or until firm. Stand cake 15 minutes; turn, top-side up, onto wire rack to cool. Dust with sifted extra cocoa to serve.
**tips** This cake can be made up to four days ahead; keep, covered, in refrigerator. Cake can also be frozen for up to three months.
**per serving** 28.2g total fat (13.2g saturated fat); 1860kJ (445 cal); 44g carbohydrate; 6.5g protein; 1.6g fibre

"This cake is divine. It tastes great on its own or even better when served warm with ice-cream. It is the only cake my mother requests."

Kelly Cruickshanks developed her love of food as a member of the Test Kitchen team, from 2000 to 2003. She now works in the commercial food industry in recipe research and development.

# raspberry hazelnut cake

**PREPARATION TIME** 30 MINUTES  **COOKING TIME** 1 HOUR 30 MINUTES (PLUS COOLING TIME)
**SERVES** 12

250g butter, softened
2 cups (440g) caster sugar
6 eggs
1 cup (150g) plain flour
½ cup (75g) self-raising flour
1 cup (100g) hazelnut meal
⅔ cup (160g) sour cream
300g fresh or frozen raspberries

## MASCARPONE CREAM

1 cup (250g) mascarpone
¼ cup (40g) icing sugar
2 tablespoons hazelnut-flavoured liqueur
½ cup (120g) sour cream
½ cup (70g) roasted hazelnuts, chopped finely

1 Preheat oven to moderate (180°C/160°C fan-forced). Grease deep 22cm-round cake pan; line base and side with baking paper.

2 Beat butter and sugar in medium bowl with electric mixer until light and fluffy; add eggs, one at a time, beating until just combined between additions. (Mixture will curdle at this stage, but will come together later.)

3 Transfer mixture to large bowl; stir in sifted flours, hazelnut meal, sour cream and raspberries. Spread mixture into pan.

4 Bake about 1½ hours. Stand cake in pan 10 minutes; turn, top-side up, onto wire rack to cool.

5 Meanwhile, make mascarpone cream.

6 Place cold cake on serving plate. Spread cake all over with mascarpone cream.
   **mascarpone cream** Combine mascarpone, icing sugar, liqueur and sour cream in medium bowl. Stir until smooth; stir in nuts.

   **tips** If using frozen raspberries, don't thaw them; frozen berries are less likely to "bleed" into the cake mixture.

   We used Frangelico in this recipe, but you can use any hazelnut-flavoured liqueur. Unfrosted cake will keep for up to three days in an airtight container at room temperature. Cake can be frosted the day before required; store, covered, in refrigerator. Unfrosted cake can be frozen for up to three months.

   **per serving** 47.9g total fat (25.3g saturated fat); 2905kJ (695 cal); 58.7g carbohydrate; 9.3g protein; 3.5g fibre

"Everyone goes wild over this cake! What's not to love?... hazelnuts, raspberries and mascarpone... food doesn't get any better than this."

Karen Hammial was the founding editor of *Australian Gourmet Traveller*, working on it for a decade before trying marketing and publishing. She returned to food and cooking, and has been food editor of the WW cookbooks for 7 years.

# carrot and banana cake

PREPARATION TIME 20 MINUTES  COOKING TIME 1 HOUR 15 MINUTES (PLUS COOLING TIME)
SERVES 10

1¼ cups (185g) plain flour

½ cup (75g) self-raising flour

1 teaspoon bicarbonate of soda

1 teaspoon mixed spice

½ teaspoon ground cinnamon

1 cup (220g) firmly packed brown sugar

¾ cup (80g) coarsely chopped walnuts

3 eggs, beaten lightly

2 cups coarsely grated carrot

1 cup mashed banana

1 cup (250ml) vegetable oil

### CREAM CHEESE FROSTING

90g packaged cream cheese

90g butter

1 cup (160g) icing sugar

1 Preheat oven to moderately slow (170°C/150°C fan-forced). Grease base and side of 24cm-round springform tin; line base with baking paper.

2 Sift flours, soda, spices and sugar into large bowl. Stir in walnuts, egg, carrot, banana and oil; pour mixture into prepared tin.

3 Bake about 1¼ hours. Cool cake in tin.

4 Meanwhile, make cream cheese frosting.

5 Top cold cake with cream cheese frosting.

**cream cheese frosting**  Beat cream cheese and butter in small bowl with electric mixer until as white as possible; gradually beat in icing sugar.

**tip**  You will need about four medium carrots (480g) and two large overripe bananas (460g) for this recipe.

Pecans can be substituted for walnuts, if desired.

**per serving**  41.5g total fat (10.6g saturated fat); 2679kJ (641 cal); 62.4g carbohydrate; 7.5g protein; 2.8g fibre

"This is so quick and easy to make, always moist, a good treat for kids and best with the cream cheese frosting."

Jodie Tilse
was one of a lively Test Kitchen team from 1994 to 1997, after which she spent four years assisting Neil Perry develop menus for Qantas. She recently helped Kylie Kwong on her new cookbook.

# vanilla butter cake

**PREPARATION TIME** 30 MINUTES  **COOKING TIME** 50 MINUTES (PLUS COOLING TIME)  **SERVES** 9

125g butter, chopped
¾ cup (180ml) milk
3 eggs
1 tablespoon vanilla extract
1 cup (220g) caster sugar
1 ½ cups (225g) self-raising flour

1 Preheat oven to moderate (180°C/160°C fan-forced). Grease deep 19cm-square cake pan; line base with baking paper.
2 Combine butter and milk in small saucepan, stir over heat until butter is melted. Remove from heat; cool to room temperature.
3 Beat eggs and extract in small bowl with electric mixer until thick and creamy; gradually add sugar, beat until dissolved between each addition.
4 Transfer mixture to large bowl, stir in half the sifted flour and half the butter mixture, then remaining flour and remaining butter mixture.
5 Pour into pan; bake about 45 minutes. Stand cake in pan 5 minutes; turn, top-side up, onto wire rack to cool. Dust cold cake with sifted icing sugar, if desired.
  **tip**  Cake can be made three days ahead; store in an airtight container.
  **per serving**  14.2g total fat (8.6g saturated fat); 1325kJ (317 cal); 43.2g carbohydrate; 5.4g protein; 1g fibre

"A good basic, light cake I often use as a base for kids' birthday cakes. Also nice plain or with cream and berries."

Jane Ash
worked in the Test Kitchen from 1986 to 1990 and has kept in touch. After an eight-year stint as a hospitality teacher, she became cookery editor for *Take 5*. She is mother to two teenagers and an eight-year-old.

# christmas fare

Your gift of choice? All the family round your table

# quince jelly

**PREPARATION TIME** 15 MINUTES  **COOKING TIME** 1 HOUR 25 MINUTES (PLUS STANDING TIME)
**MAKES** ABOUT 5 CUPS

6 large quinces (2kg)
1.75 litres (7 cups) water
5 cups (1.1kg) white sugar, approximately
½ cup (125ml) lemon juice, strained

1 Chop unpeeled, uncored quinces coarsely.
2 Combine quince and the water in large saucepan, bring to a boil; reduce heat, simmer, covered, about 1 hour or until quince is soft.
3 Strain mixture through fine cloth; stand overnight. Allow liquid to drip through cloth slowly, do not squeeze cloth; discard pulp.
4 Measure quince liquid. Allow one cup of sugar for each cup of quince liquid.
5 Combine quince liquid and sugar in large saucepan. Stir over heat, without boiling, until sugar is dissolved. Stir in juice, bring to a boil; boil, uncovered, without stirring, about 25 minutes or until jelly sets when tested on a cold saucer.
6 Pour jelly into hot sterilised jars; seal while hot.
  **tips** Store jelly in a cool, dark place for up to 12 months.
  Refrigerate jelly once opened.
  **per tablespoon** 0.0g total fat (0.0g saturated fat); 343kJ (82 cal); 20.9g carbohydrate; 0.1g protein; 1.7g fibre

"This is my family's all-time favourite. I make enough to last the whole year – and give as Christmas presents."
Louise Patniotis is the food editor who compiled the recipes in this book. After 18 years in the Test Kitchen, she "still loves it!" and works producing the WW mini and maxi cookbooks. She is married and the mother of two sons.

# chocolate nut slice

**PREPARATION TIME** 15 MINUTES (PLUS REFRIGERATION TIME)  **MAKES** 18

½ x 395g can sweetened condensed milk
250g dark eating chocolate, melted
½ cup (70g) coarsely chopped roasted hazelnuts
½ cup (60g) coarsely chopped roasted pecans
½ cup (80g) coarsely chopped roasted blanched almonds

1 Grease 8cm x 26cm bar cake pan; line base and sides with baking paper,
  extending paper 5cm above long sides.
2 Combine ingredients in medium bowl. Spread mixture into pan.
3 Refrigerate several hours or overnight until firm.

**tips** Any combination of nuts can be used.
Slice can be kept, wrapped in plastic wrap and refrigerated, for up to four weeks.

**per serving** 13.2g total fat (4.1g saturated fat); 907kJ (217 cal); 21.4g carbohydrate;
4.3g protein; 1.2g fibre

"Quick and easy to make – great for gifts and delicious to serve with coffee."
Sally Kennard
was part of the team who put together the first WW soft-cover cookbook, *Best Ever Recipes*. In 1982, Sally and her family moved to Wagga Wagga where, for 23 years, she's taught commercial cookery.

# fruit mince pies

**PREPARATION TIME** (PLUS STANDING AND REFRIGERATION TIME) **COOKING TIME** 25 MINUTES
**MAKES** 24

2 cups (300g) plain flour

150g butter, chopped

1 teaspoon finely grated orange rind

1 tablespoon vegetable oil

2 tablespoons caster sugar

1 egg, beaten lightly

1 tablespoon iced water, approximately

1 egg, beaten lightly, extra

SPICED FRUIT MINCE

1 cup (160g) sultanas

1¼ cups (185g) raisins, chopped

¾ cup (120g) dried currants

¾ cup (110g) seeded dates, chopped coarsely

1 cup (170g) seeded prunes, chopped coarsely

1 small green-skinned apple (130g), peeled, grated

¼ cup (55g) firmly packed brown sugar

2 teaspoons finely grated orange rind

1 teaspoon mixed spice

½ teaspoon ground clove

2 tablespoons plum jam

⅓ cup (80ml) brandy

1 Make spiced fruit mince.

2 Sift flour into medium bowl, rub in butter; stir in rind, oil and sugar (or process flour, butter, rind, oil and sugar until crumbly).

3 Add egg and enough water to make ingredients cling together. Turn onto floured surface; knead until smooth. Cover pastry; refrigerate 30 minutes.

4 Preheat oven to moderate (180°C/160°C fan-forced). Lightly grease two 12-hole (2 tablespoons/40ml) patty pan trays.

5 Roll two-thirds of the pastry between sheets of baking paper until 3mm thick. Cut 24 x 7.5cm rounds from pastry.

6 Place rounds into pan holes. Divide fruit mince among pastry cases. Roll remaining pastry between sheets of baking paper until 3mm thick. Cut 12 x 5cm rounds from remaining pastry. Cut small stars from each round. Top half the pies with the rounds; top remaining pies with the star cut-outs. Brush pastry rounds and stars with extra beaten egg.

7 Bake about 25 minutes or until browned. Transfer to wire rack to cool. Serve dusted with sifted icing sugar, if desired.

**spiced fruit mince** Mix ingredients in large bowl. Cover tightly with plastic wrap. Refrigerate for three days before using; stir mixture once a day. You will need 2½ cups (500g) of the spiced fruit mince for the pies. The remaining mince can be kept, covered, in the refrigerator for up to six months, or double the pastry recipe to make 48 pies.

**per serving** 6.6g total fat (3.7g saturated fat); 890kJ (213 cal); 34.7g carbohydrate; 2.7g protein; 2.6g fibre

# gourmet rocky road

**PREPARATION TIME** 20 MINUTES (PLUS REFRIGERATION TIME) **SERVES** 20

300g toasted marshmallows with coconut, chopped coarsely
400g turkish delight, chopped coarsely
¼ cup (40g) roasted blanched almonds, chopped coarsely
½ cup (70g) roasted pistachios
450g white eating chocolate, melted

1 Grease two 8cm x 26cm bar cake pans; line base and sides with baking paper, extending paper 5cm above long sides.
2 Combine marshmallow, turkish delight and nuts in large bowl. Working quickly, stir in chocolate; spread mixture into pans, push down firmly to flatten the top. Refrigerate until set.

**tip** Rocky road will keep in the refrigerator for up to four weeks.

**per serving** 10.4g total fat (5g saturated fat); 1041kJ (249 cal); 39.5g carbohydrate; 3.4g protein; 0.5g fibre

"Everyone who tries this sweet, loves it. I adore the turkish delight in it."
Susie Riggall
graduated from university and turned to finance before cooking excited her interest. After a year in the Test Kitchen, she left to pursue a career as a personal chef.

"With the white choc, turkish delight and pistachios, you have a rocky road to please even the most mature adult."
Nancy Duran
turned from advertising in her native US to become a chef in top restaurants in Sydney and New York. She joined the Test Kitchen team in 2003 before leaving in 2004 to become an assistant food editor on a food magazine.

# grand marnier fruit cake

**PREPARATION TIME** 1 HOUR (PLUS STANDING TIME)

**COOKING TIME** 3 HOURS 45 MINUTES (PLUS COOLING TIME)  **SERVES** 36

3 cups (480g) sultanas

1½ cups (250g) mixed peel

¾ cup (110g) coarsely chopped raisins

¾ cup (120g) coarsely chopped seeded dried dates

⅔ cup (140g) coarsely chopped seeded prunes

½ cup (125g) coarsely chopped glacé apricots

⅔ cup (150g) coarsely chopped glacé pineapple

½ cup (70g) slivered almonds

½ cup (60g) coarsely chopped walnuts

1 tablespoon finely grated orange rind

½ cup (110g) caster sugar

¼ cup (60ml) orange juice

½ cup (125ml) Grand Marnier

250g butter, softened

½ cup (110g) firmly packed brown sugar

5 eggs

2 cups (300g) plain flour

2 tablespoons Grand Marnier, extra

1 Combine all of the fruit in a large jar or large container with a tight-fitting lid; mix in nuts and rind.

2 Sprinkle caster sugar evenly into medium heavy-based frying pan. Cook, over low heat, without stirring, until sugar begins to melt; at that point, immediately begin stirring until sugar is completely melted and golden brown. Remove from heat, stir in orange juice. Return to heat, stirring constantly, until toffee-like pieces have dissolved. Do not boil or mixture will evaporate. Stir in liqueur then strain into jug; discard any small pieces of toffee. Pour over fruit mixture; cover tightly with plastic wrap or lid.

3 Next day, turn jar upside down or stir fruit well; do this daily for 10 days.

4 On the day of baking, preheat oven to slow (150°C/130°C fan-forced). Grease deep 22cm-round or deep 19cm-square cake pan; line base and side(s) of pan with four thicknesses of baking paper, extending paper 5cm above edge(s).

5 Beat butter and brown sugar in small bowl with electric mixer until combined; add eggs, one at a time, beating until just combined between additions. Pour fruit mixture into large bowl; add egg mixture, mix with hand. Add sifted flour; mix well with hand.

6 Spread mixture into pan. Bake about 3½ hours. Brush top of hot cake with extra liqueur, cover with foil; cool in pan overnight.

**tip** Cake can be made six months ahead; store in an airtight container, in the refrigerator, or freeze for up to 12 months.

**per serving** 8.9g total fat (4.1g saturated fat); 1053kJ (252 cal); 39.7g carbohydrate; 3.2g protein; 2.2g fibre

"In 1982, food editor Ellen Sinclair asked me to make up a rich fruit cake using Grand Marnier. I made it for my son's wedding cake."

Pamela Clark became senior home economist in the Test Kitchen in 1969. After a time in Tasmania, working as a presenter on radio and TV, she came back to the Test Kitchen in 1978. She is currently ACP Test Kitchen director.

# frozen chocolate fruit cake pudding

PREPARATION TIME 40 MINUTES (PLUS STANDING TIME)

COOKING TIME 10 MINUTES (PLUS REFRIGERATION AND FREEZING TIME) **SERVES** 10

½ cup (95g) coarsely chopped dried figs

¼ cup (40g) coarsely chopped raisins

¼ cup (45g) coarsely chopped dried prunes

¼ cup (50g) coarsely chopped glacé cherries

4 fresh dates (100g), seeded, chopped coarsely

2 teaspoons finely grated orange rind

½ cup (125ml) brandy

125g butter

½ cup (75g) plain flour

½ cup (110g) firmly packed brown sugar

1 cup (250ml) milk

600ml thickened cream

⅔ cup (220g) hazelnut spread

1 teaspoon ground nutmeg

1 teaspoon ground cinnamon

4 egg yolks

⅓ cup (45g) roasted hazelnuts, chopped coarsely

200g dark eating chocolate, chopped finely

200g dark eating chocolate, melted, extra

1 Combine fruit, rind and brandy in large bowl; mix well. Cover tightly with plastic wrap; store in a cool, dark place for up to a week, stirring every day.

2 Line 17.5cm, 1.75-litre (7-cup) pudding basin with plastic wrap, extending plastic 5cm over edge.

3 Melt butter in medium saucepan, add flour; stir over heat until bubbling. Remove from heat; stir in sugar then milk and half of the cream. Stir over medium heat until mixture boils and thickens. Transfer to large bowl; stir in spread, spices and egg yolks. Cover surface of mixture with plastic wrap; refrigerate 1 hour.

4 Stir in fruit mixture, nuts and chopped chocolate. Beat remaining cream in small bowl with electric mixer until soft peaks form; fold into pudding mixture. Spoon mixture into basin, tap basin lightly to remove air bubbles. Cover with foil; freeze overnight.

5 Turn pudding onto tray; remove plastic wrap, return pudding to freezer.

6 Cut a 35cm circle from a piece of paper to use as a guide; cover paper with plastic wrap. Spread melted chocolate over plastic wrap then quickly drape plastic, chocolate-side down, over pudding. Quickly smooth with hands, avoiding deep pleats in the plastic. Freeze until firm. Peel away plastic; trim away excess chocolate. Serve with a selection of fresh fruit, if desired.

**tip** Pudding can be made up to one week ahead.

**per serving** 57.2g total fat (31.8g saturated fat); 3566kJ (853 cal); 73.8g carbohydrate; 9g protein; 3.9g fibre

"A lot of Aussies prefer to have a cold Christmas dinner, these days. If you fit into that category, this is the pudding recipe for you."

Pamela Clark was appointed food editor of both the WW magazine and cookbooks in 1984. Since then, she has written and/or edited more than 200 ACP cookbooks. In 1999, Pamela was appointed ACP Test Kitchen director, a position she still enjoys.

# lyndey's boiled fruit cake

**PREPARATION TIME** 45 MINUTES  **COOKING TIME** 3 HOURS 10 MINUTES (PLUS COOLING TIME)
**SERVES** 36

3 cups (450g) raisins, chopped coarsely
1½ cups (240g) sultanas
¾ cup (120g) dried currants
½ cup (100g) red glacé cherries, chopped coarsely
¼ cup (60ml) brandy
250g butter, chopped
1 cup (250ml) water
½ cup (110g) firmly packed dark brown sugar
½ cup (110g) caster sugar
½ teaspoon bicarbonate of soda
4 eggs, beaten lightly
1¼ cups (185g) self-raising flour
1¼ cups (185g) plain flour
1 cup (120g) pecans
¾ cup (100g) macadamias
¼ cup (60ml) brandy, extra

1 Combine fruit, brandy, butter, the water, sugars and soda in large saucepan; stir over medium heat until butter is melted and sugar dissolved. Bring to a boil, remove from heat, transfer to large bowl; cool to room temperature.

2 Preheat oven to slow (150°C/130°C fan-forced). Grease deep 22cm-round or deep 19cm-square cake pan; line base and side(s) of pan with two thicknesses of baking paper, extending paper 5cm above edge(s).

3 Stir egg into fruit mixture, then stir in sifted flours; spread evenly into pan. Decorate top with nuts. Bake about 3 hours.

4 Brush hot cake with extra brandy. Cover hot cake with foil; cool in pan overnight.

**tips** Dates, prunes, apricots or nuts can be substituted for the red glacé cherries, if you prefer.

Cake can be made up to six months ahead; store in an airtight container in the refrigerator, or freeze for up to 12 months.

**per serving** 11.1g total fat (4.4g saturated fat); 1003kJ (240 cal); 31.6g carbohydrate; 3g protein; 2g fibre

"My mother, Isabel Hall, first made this cake (without the generous quantity of fruit and nuts) in the war years to send to troops overseas. The recipe was given to her by her mother-in-law when she married in 1940. She embellished it for my brother's 21st birthday in 1963. Since then, it has become a family favourite. Here, we reprint it in memory of my mother."

Lyndey Milan joined the WW as food director in 1999. She is also co-host of TV's *Fresh with The Australian Women's Weekly*, on the Nine Network in Australia and Prime in New Zealand – and mother of two grown children.

"This is a favourite and my mum cooks it, too. It's rich and fruity and moist, all the things a good fruit cake should be."

Jan Purser (formerly Castorina) worked in the Test Kitchen for six years (1987-1993), as chief home economist and then deputy food editor. Jan helped plan and edit cookbooks, the menu planner series and the quick and easy series. She now lives in Perth, WA.

# celebration cake

**PREPARATION TIME** 50 MINUTES (PLUS STANDING TIME)
**COOKING TIME** 3 HOURS 30 MINUTES (PLUS COOLING TIME) **SERVES** 36

3 cups (500g) sultanas
1½ cups (250g) coarsely chopped raisins
1½ cups (250g) coarsely chopped dates
¾ cup (120g) dried currants
½ cup (85g) mixed peel
⅔ cup (140g) quartered glacé cherries
¼ cup (55g) coarsely chopped glacé pineapple
¼ cup (60g) coarsely chopped glacé apricots
½ cup (125ml) rum
250g butter, softened
1 cup (220g) firmly packed brown sugar
5 eggs
1½ cups (225g) plain flour
⅓ cup (50g) self-raising flour
1 teaspoon mixed spice

1 Combine fruit in large bowl with rum. Cover tightly with plastic wrap; store in a cool, dark place overnight or up to a week, stirring every day.

2 On the day of baking, preheat oven to slow (150°C/130°C fan-forced). Grease deep 22cm-round or deep 19cm-square cake pan; line base and side(s) of pan with four thicknesses of baking paper, extending paper 5cm above edge(s).

3 Beat butter in medium bowl with electric mixer until soft, add sugar, beat only until combined. Add eggs, one at a time, beat only until combined. Add creamed mixture to fruit mixture; mix well. Stir in sifted dry ingredients.

4 Spread mixture evenly into pan. Bake about 3½ hours. Cover hot cake with foil; cool in pan overnight.

**tip** Cake can be made six months ahead; store in an airtight container, in the refrigerator, or freeze for up to 12 months.

**per serving** 6.7g total fat (4g saturated fat); 966kJ (231 cal); 39.8g carbohydrate; 2.6g protein; 2.2g fibre

# rich sherried fruit cake

PREPARATION TIME 30 MINUTES (PLUS STANDING TIME)
COOKING TIME UP TO 3 HOURS 15 MINUTES DEPENDING ON CAKE PAN SIZE (PLUS COOLING TIME)
SERVES 36

"This is a real favourite at Christmas time. It is extremely easy and tastes delicious."

Elizabeth Hooper worked in the Test Kitchen for 13 years, the last few of which were spent as Test Kitchen manager. She left in 2001 to pursue study and embark on a career change.

250g butter, softened
2 tablespoons plum jam
2 teaspoons finely grated orange rind
1¼ cups (275g) firmly packed brown sugar
5 eggs
¾ cup (180ml) sweet sherry
1½ cups (225g) plain flour
½ cup (75g) self-raising flour
2 teaspoons mixed spice
1kg (5 cups) mixed dried fruit
½ cup (125ml) sweet sherry, extra

1 Preheat oven to slow (150°C/130°C fan-forced). Grease base of chosen pan (see below); line base and side(s) with four thicknesses of baking paper, extending paper 5cm above edge(s).

2 Beat butter, jam, rind and sugar in medium bowl with electric mixer until just combined. Add eggs, one at a time, beating between additions until just combined.

3 Stir in ½ cup of the sherry, sifted dry ingredients and fruit; mix well.

4 Spread mixture into pan. Bake for time specified below.

5 Brush top of hot cake with remaining ¼ cup sherry, cover hot cake with foil; cool in pan overnight.

6 Remove cake from pan, remove paper from cake. Brush cake all over with 2 tablespoons of the warmed extra sherry each week for 3 weeks.

tips Cake can be made up to three months ahead; store in an airtight container in the refrigerator, or freeze for up to 12 months.

cake pan sizes and cooking times

1 x deep 22cm-round or deep 19cm-square cake pan – cook 3¼ hours

2 x deep 17cm-round or deep 15cm-square cake pans – cook 2 hours

4 x deep 12.5cm-round or deep 9.5cm-square cake pans – cook 1¾ hours

per serving 6.8g total fat (4.1g saturated fat); 869kJ (208 cal); 33.5g carbohydrate; 2.4g protein; 1.9 g fibre

# boiled Christmas pudding

PREPARATION TIME 30 MINUTES (PLUS STANDING TIME)
COOKING TIME 6 HOURS (PLUS COOLING TIME) SERVES 12

1½ cups (225g) raisins
1½ cups (240g) sultanas
1 cup (150g) dried currants
¾ cup (120g) mixed peel
1 teaspoon finely grated lemon rind
2 tablespoons lemon juice
2 tablespoons brandy
250g butter, softened
2 cups (440g) firmly packed brown sugar
5 eggs
1¼ cups (185g) plain flour
1 teaspoon mixed spice
4 cups (280g) stale breadcrumbs

1 Combine fruit, rind, juice and brandy in large bowl. Cover tightly with plastic wrap; store in a cool, dark place overnight or up to a week, stirring every day.

2 Beat butter and sugar in large bowl with electric mixer until just combined. Beat in eggs, one at a time, beat only until combined between each addition. Add butter mixture to fruit mixture then add sifted dry ingredients and breadcrumbs; mix well.

3 Fill large boiler three-quarters full of hot water, cover; bring to a boil. Have ready 2.5m of kitchen string and an extra ½ cup of plain flour. Wearing thick rubber gloves, dip pudding cloth in boiling water; boil 1 minute then remove, carefully squeeze excess water from cloth. Working quickly, spread hot cloth on bench, rub flour into centre of cloth to cover an area about 40cm in diameter, leaving flour a little thicker in centre of cloth where "skin" on the pudding needs to be thickest.

4 Place pudding mixture in centre of cloth. Gather cloth evenly around mixture. Tie cloth tightly with string as close to mixture as possible. Knot two pairs of corners together to make pudding easier to remove.

5 Lower pudding into boiling water; tie free ends of string to handles of boiler to suspend pudding. Cover with tight-fitting lid, boil for 6 hours, replenishing water as necessary. Lift pudding from water. Suspend from a wooden spoon by placing over rungs of upturned stool or wedging handle in drawer. Hang 10 minutes.

6 Place pudding on board; cut string, carefully peel back cloth. Turn pudding onto a plate then carefully peel cloth away completely; cool. Stand at least 20 minutes or until skin darkens and pudding becomes firm.

tips You need a 60cm-square of unbleached calico for the cloth. If calico is new, soak in cold water overnight; next day, boil 20 minutes then rinse.

to store pudding Wrap cold pudding in plastic wrap and seal tightly in a freezer bag or airtight container. Pudding can be stored in refrigerator up to two months or frozen up to 12 months.

to reheat pudding Thaw frozen pudding three days in refrigerator; remove from refrigerator 12 hours before reheating. Remove plastic wrap; tie dry unfloured cloth around pudding. Boil 2 hours, following instructions above.

per serving 20.6g total fat (12.2g saturated fat); 2658kJ (636 cal); 104.9g carbohydrate; 9.2g protein; 4.3g fibre

"I make this pudding every Christmas for my family, not to mention extra puds for various friends; it is a real winner."
Pamela Clark first worked in the Test Kitchen in 1969 as senior home economist where she stayed until 1973. She returned in 1978, and was appointed WW food editor in 1984. Pamela became ACP Test Kitchen director in 1999, she also appears regularly on TV in *Fresh with The Australian Women's Weekly* on the Nine Network.

# super-rich chocolate Drambuie fruit cake

**PREPARATION TIME** 50 MINUTES (PLUS STANDING TIME)

**COOKING TIME** 4 HOURS 30 MINUTES (PLUS COOLING TIME)  **SERVES** 36

2⅓ cups (375g) sultanas

2¼ cups (375g) raisins, chopped coarsely

1⅔ cups (230g) dried currants

1½ cups (250g) prunes, seeded, chopped coarsely

1½ cups (210g) dried dates, seeded, chopped coarsely

¾ cup (120g) mixed peel

⅔ cup (140g) red glacé cherries, quartered

1⅓ cups (330ml) Drambuie

⅓ cup (115g) honey

1 tablespoon finely grated lemon rind

250g butter, softened

1½ cups (330g) firmly packed dark brown sugar

6 eggs

90g dark eating chocolate, grated

1¼ cups (150g) pecans, chopped

2 cups (300g) plain flour

1 cup (150g) self-raising flour

¼ cup (25g) cocoa powder

1 Combine fruit, 1 cup (250ml) of the Drambuie, honey and rind in large bowl. Cover tightly with plastic wrap; store in a cool, dark place overnight or up to a week, stirring every day.

2 On the day of baking, preheat oven to very slow (120°C/100°C fan-forced). Grease six-hole (¾-cup/180ml) texas-style muffin pan. Grease deep 22cm-round or deep 19cm-square cake pan; line base and side(s) with four thicknesses of baking paper, extending paper 5cm above edge(s).

3 Beat butter and sugar in medium bowl with electric mixer until just combined. Add eggs, one at a time, beating until combined between additions. Stir into fruit mixture with chocolate and nuts. Stir in sifted dry ingredients, in two batches.

4 Fill each hole of muffin pan, level to the top, with mixture; spread remaining mixture into cake pan. Decorate tops with extra pecans and glacé cherries, if desired.

5 Bake muffins 1½ hours (cake can stand while muffins are baking). Brush hot muffins with some of the remaining Drambuie; cover with foil, cool in pan.

6 Increase oven temperature to slow (150°C/130°C fan-forced). Bake large cake 3 hours. Brush hot cake with remaining Drambuie; cover hot cake with foil; cool in pan overnight.

**tips** You can make a larger cake by using a deep 25cm-round or deep 23cm-square cake pan, if you prefer; allow about 4 to 4½ hours for baking.

Cake can be made up to three months ahead; store in an airtight container in the refrigerator, or freeze for up to 12 months.

**per serving** 12.3g total fat (5.7g saturated fat); 1471kJ (352 cal); 55.5g carbohydrate; 4.5g protein; 3.4g fibre

"Weeks before the cakes are baked, I make triple quantity of the macerated fruit mix... as much of it disappears during sampling."

Janene Brooks enjoyed her time in the Test Kitchen from 1994 to 1996. Moving home to Melbourne, she continued in the food industry, had a child, then decided to study interior design.

# delectably rich fruit cake

**PREPARATION TIME** 40 MINUTES (PLUS STANDING TIME)
**COOKING TIME** 2 HOURS (PLUS COOLING TIME  **SERVES** 36

⅓ cup (55g) seeded prunes, halved

1½ cups (240g) sultanas

1½ cups (230g) dried currants

½ cup (125ml) sweet sherry

½ cup (125ml) brandy

125g butter, softened

½ cup (110g) firmly packed brown sugar

3 eggs

1 tablespoon instant coffee granules

¼ cup (60ml) hot water

¼ cup (80g) plum jam

1 cup (150g) plain flour

¾ cup (110g) self-raising flour

1 tablespoon cocoa powder

1 teaspoon ground cinnamon

½ teaspoon mixed spice

½ teaspoon ground nutmeg

1½ cups (300g) glacé cherries

1½ cups (250g) halved, seeded dates

1 cup (170g) mixed peel

2 cups (240g) coarsely chopped walnuts

"This is the best fruitcake I have ever tasted – I have made it every Christmas for the past 20 years!"

Jo Anne Calabria (nee Power) is a food editor, writer and food consultant. She worked in the Test Kitchen from 1985 until 1987, was a magazine food editor for 10 years and is now a food consultant.

1 Combine prunes, sultanas and currants in large bowl, stir in sherry and brandy. Cover tightly with plastic wrap; store in a cool, dark place overnight or up to a week, stirring every day.

2 On the day of baking, preheat oven to slow (150°C/130°C fan-forced). Grease deep 22cm-round or deep 19cm-square cake pan; line base and side(s) of pan with four thicknesses of baking paper, extending paper 5cm above edge(s).

3 Beat butter and sugar in small bowl with electric mixer only until combined. Add eggs quickly, one at a time, beat only until combined between each addition.

4 Transfer mixture to large bowl; stir in the combined coffee and the water and jam, then the sifted dry ingredients in two batches. Drain prune mixture, reserve liquid. Add prune mixture, cherries, dates, peel and walnuts to cake mixture.

5 Spread mixture into pan. Bake about 2 hours.

6 Brush reserved prune liquid over hot cake; cover with foil, cool in pan overnight.

**tips** Fruit for soaking can be prepared up to two weeks ahead.

Cake can be made up to three months ahead; store in an airtight container in the refrigerator, or freeze for up to 12 months.

**per serving**  8.1g total fat (2.3g saturated fat); 936kJ (224 cal); 33.3g carbohydrate; 3g protein; 2.4g fibre

# irish pudding cake

**PREPARATION TIME** 25 MINUTES (PLUS STANDING TIME)
**COOKING TIME** 3 HOURS (PLUS COOLING TIME) **SERVES** 16

1½ cups (210g) seeded dried dates, chopped coarsely
1¼ cups (210g) seeded prunes, chopped coarsely
1½ cups (225g) raisins, chopped coarsely
1 cup (110g) dried currants
¾ cup (120g) sultanas
1 large apple (200g), grated coarsely
1½ cups (375ml) Irish whiskey
1¼ cups (275g) firmly packed dark brown sugar
185g butter, softened
3 eggs, beaten lightly
½ cup (50g) hazelnut meal
1½ cups (225g) plain flour
1 teaspoon ground nutmeg
½ teaspoon ground ginger
½ teaspoon ground cloves
½ teaspoon bicarbonate of soda

1 Combine fruit and 1 cup of the whiskey in large bowl, cover tightly with plastic wrap; stand at room temperature overnight.

2 Preheat oven to very slow (120°C/100°C fan-forced). Grease deep 20cm-round cake pan; line base and side of pan with two thicknesses of baking paper, extending paper 5cm above side.

3 Combine remaining whiskey and ½ cup of the sugar in small saucepan. Stir over heat until sugar dissolves; bring to a boil. Remove from heat; cool syrup 20 minutes.

4 Meanwhile, beat butter and remaining sugar in small bowl with electric mixer until just combined (do not overbeat). Add eggs, one at a time, beating until just combined between additions. Add butter mixture to fruit mixture; stir in hazelnut meal, sifted dry ingredients and ½ cup of the cooled syrup.

5 Spread mixture into pan. Bake about 3 hours. Brush cake with reheated remaining syrup; cover hot cake with foil, cool in pan overnight.

tips If your dilemma is whether to make a Christmas cake or pudding, this recipe is the best of both worlds because it's just as delicious served hot as a pudding or cold as a cake. And it's not necessary to make it ages in advance: starting to prepare it a day or so ahead is just fine.

Cake will keep, covered, in the refrigerator for up to a month.

Although the inclusion of Irish whiskey makes it authentic, scotch, dark rum or brandy are fine substitutes.

**per serving** 12.8g total fat (6.7g saturated fat); 177kJ (425 cal); 62.8g carbohydrate; 4.7g protein; 4.8g fibre

"We released one of our famous WW cookbooks called *Christmas Cooking* in 2004, with lots of our most requested recipes, and some brand new ones. Among the 'new' is an idea of mine to turn the popular Irish Fruit Cake recipe into a cross between a cake and a pudding. The result is sublime."

Pamela Clark became senior home economist in the Test Kitchen in 1969. After a time in Tasmania, working as a presenter on radio and TV, she came back to the Test Kitchen in 1978 and, in 1984, was appointed food editor of the WW magazine and cookbooks. Since then, she has written and/or edited more than 200 ACP cookbooks. In 1999, Pamela was appointed ACP Test Kitchen director. She appears regularly in *Fresh with The Australian Women's Weekly* on the Nine Network.

"At Christmas I often make the chocolate Christmas tree. However, I now make it with a rocky road mixture."

Rosemary Wellington worked in the Test Kitchen in the late 1970s. She left to cook at Crank's Restaurant in London and test recipes for their cookbook. She now makes menswear in Melbourne – and still cooks.

# chocolate hazelnut Christmas tree

**PREPARATION TIME** 30 MINUTES (PLUS REFRIGERATION TIME)

Bring out this tree with the coffee, suggesting to your guests that they snap off bits of the branches. Or, for an impressive gift, wrap the whole tree in cellophane and deliver it on the day.

24cm-round covered cake board
500g dark eating chocolate, melted
2 cups (240g) finely chopped roasted hazelnuts
60g dark eating chocolate, extra
1 brazil nut
2 teaspoons icing sugar

1 Grease four oven trays; line each with baking paper. Mark nine crosses, measuring 7cm, 9cm, 11cm, 13cm, 14cm, 15cm, 16cm, 17cm and 18cm on trays, leaving about 3cm space between each cross. Mark an 18cm cross on cake board.

2 Combine chocolate and hazelnuts in medium bowl. Drop teaspoonfuls of the chocolate mixture along all the marked crosses to make branches; refrigerate several hours or overnight.

3 Drop about a teaspoon of the extra melted chocolate into the centre of the 18cm cross on cake board; position the 18cm branch on top, moving it around until the best position is found.

4 Assemble the remaining eight branches in pairs, starting from the largest remaining branch and finishing with the smallest, using about a teaspoon of the extra melted chocolate in the centre of each crossed pair; refrigerate until set.

5 Secure each pair to the next with a little melted chocolate (if the branches look a little uneven, support them underneath with a match box). Secure brazil nut to centre of smallest branch with a little melted chocolate; drizzle remaining melted chocolate over nut to cover it in chocolate. Refrigerate until chocolate sets between branches. Store tree in refrigerator until required; dust with sifted icing sugar.

   **tip** This tree takes a little time to make, but it is delightful to look at and delicious to eat. The Christmas tree can be made two days ahead.

# glossary

**allspice** also known as pimento or jamaican pepper.

**bacon rasher** slices of bacon.

**basil** an aromatic herb; there are many types, but the most commonly used is sweet basil.
**opal** also known as purple basil; has large purple leaves and a sweet, almost gingery flavour.
**thai** also known as horapa; has smallish leaves and a sweet licorice/aniseed taste. Available in Asian supermarkets and greengrocers.

**bean sprouts** tender new growths of assorted beans and seeds.

**burghul** also known as bulghur wheat; hulled steamed wheat kernels. Not the same as cracked wheat.

**butter** use salted or unsalted (sweet) butter; 125g is equal to 1 stick butter.

**buttermilk** sold in the refrigerated dairy compartments in supermarkets. Originally just the liquid left after cream was separated from milk, today it is commercially made similarly to yogurt.

**capsicum** also known as bell pepper or, simply, pepper.

**cardamom** purchase in pod, seed or ground form. Has a distinctive aromatic, sweetly rich flavour.

**cheese**
**bocconcini** baby mozzarella, a delicate, semi-soft, white cheese.
**cottage** fresh, white, unripened curd cheese with a grainy consistency.
**cream cheese** commonly known as Philadelphia or Philly, a soft cow-milk cheese.
**fetta** a crumbly textured goat or sheep-milk cheese with a sharp, salty taste.
**gorgonzola** a creamy blue cheese having a mild, sweet taste.
**mascarpone** a cultured cream product made similarly to yogurt. Is whitish to creamy yellow in colour, with a soft, creamy texture.
**mozzarella** soft, spun-curd cheese.
**parmesan** also known as parmigiano; is a hard, grainy cow-milk cheese.

**ricotta** soft white cow-milk cheese; Is a sweet, moist cheese with a slightly grainy texture.

**chickpeas** also called garbanzos, hummus or channa; an irregularly round, sandy-coloured legume.

**chilli** use rubber gloves when seeding and chopping fresh chillies as they can burn your skin. Removing seeds and membranes lessens the heat level.
**powder** made from dried ground thai chillies.
**red thai** small, medium hot, and bright red in colour.

**chinese broccoli** also known as gai larn, kanah, gai lum and chinese kale; appreciated more for its stems than its coarse leaves.

**chinese cabbage** also known as peking or napa cabbage, wong bok or petsai. Elongated in shape with pale green, crinkly leaves.

**chinese cooking wine** also called chinese rice wine. Mirin or sherry can be substituted.

**chocolate** we used eating quality milk, dark and white chocolate.
**choc bits** also known as chocolate chips and chocolate morsels.
**chocolate Melts** discs of compounded chocolate ideal for melting.

**chorizo** a sausage made of coarsely ground pork and highly seasoned with garlic and chillies.

**choy sum** also known as pakaukeo or flowering cabbage, a member of the bok choy family; has long stems, light green leaves and yellow flowers. Is eaten, stems and all.

**cocoa powder** also known as cocoa; dried, unsweetened, roasted ground cocoa beans.

**coriander** also known as pak chee, cilantro or chinese parsley; the stems, roots and leaves are used. Also available as seeds or ground.

**cornflour** also known as cornstarch; used as a thickening agent in cooking.

**cornichon** French for gherkin, a very small variety of cucumber.

**couscous** a fine, grain-like cereal product made from semolina.

**cucumber**
**lebanese** long, slender and thin-skinned; also known as european or burpless cucumber.
**telegraph** long and green with ridges running down its entire length; also known as continental cucumber.

**cumin** also known as zeera.

**currants, dried** tiny, almost black raisins so-named after a grape variety.

**custard powder** instant mixture used to make pouring custard.

**eggplant** also known as aubergine.

**eggs** some recipes in this book call for raw or barely cooked eggs; exercise caution if there is a salmonella problem in your area.

**evaporated milk** unsweetened canned milk from which water has been extracted by evaporation.

**five-spice powder** a mixture of ground cinnamon, cloves, star anise, sichuan pepper and fennel seeds.

**garam masala** based on varying proportions of cardamom, cinnamon, cloves, coriander, fennel and cumin, roasted and ground together.

**gelatine** we used powdered gelatine; also available in sheet form known as leaf gelatine.

**ghee** clarified butter; can be heated to a high temperature without burning.

**ginger, fresh** also known as green or root ginger; ground ginger cannot be substituted.
**ground** also known as powdered ginger; used as a flavouring in cakes.

**golden syrup** a by-product of refined sugarcane; pure maple syrup or honey can be substituted.

**jam** also known as preserve or conserve; usually made from fruit.

**kaffir lime leaves** also known as bai magrood; a strip of fresh lime peel can be substituted for each kaffir lime leaf.

**kecap manis** a dark, thick sweet soy sauce.

**kumara** Polynesian name of orange-fleshed sweet potato often confused with yam.

**lebanese bread** also known as pitta bread; flat pieces that separate into two thin rounds.

**lemon grass** a lemon-smelling and tasting, sharp-edged grass; the white lower part of the stem is used.

**mesclun** a salad mix of assorted young lettuce and other green leaves.

**mirin** a japanese champagne-coloured cooking wine expressly for cooking – do not confuse with sake.

**mixed peel** candied citrus peel.

**mortadella** delicately spiced and smoked italian pressed pork and beef.

**noodles**
**bean thread** also known as glass or cellophane noodles because they are transparent when cooked.
**shirataki** a Japanese translucent jelly-like noodle made from starch of konnyaku, a yam-like root vegetable. Available in refrigerated packets. Closest dry substitute is rice vermicelli.
**fried** crispy egg noodles packaged already deep-fried.
**vermicelli** also known as sen mee, mei fun or bee hoon. Used in spring rolls and cold salads.

**paprika** ground, dried red capsicum (bell pepper), available sweet, hot or smoked.

**parsley, flat-leaf** also known as italian or continental parsley.

**pine nuts** also known as pignoli.

**polenta** also known as cornmeal; a flour-like cereal made of dried corn (maize) sold ground in several different textures; also the name of the dish made from it.

**prawns** also known as shrimp.

**prosciutto** salt-cured, air-dried (unsmoked) pressed ham; usually sold in paper-thin slices, ready to eat.

**raddicchio** a type of lettuce with dark burgundy leaves and a strong bitter flavour.

**rice**
**arborio** small, round-grain rice especially suitable for risottos.
**basmati** a white, fragrant long-grained rice. It should be washed several times before cooking.
**koshihikari** a Japanese rice perfect for sushi; available from supermarkets.

**rice paper sheets** also known as banh trang. Made from rice paste and stamped into rounds.

**sambal oelek** also ulek or olek; Indonesian in origin; a salty paste made from ground chillies and vinegar.

**sauces**
**char siu** a chinese barbecue sauce made from sugar, water, salt, honey, fermented soybean paste, soy sauce, malt syrup and spices. It can be found at most supermarkets.
**fish** made from pulverised salted fermented fish (most often anchovies); has a pungent smell and strong taste, so use according to your taste.
**oyster** a rich, brown sauce made from oysters and their brine.
**soy** also known as sieu, is made from fermented soy beans. We used a mild Japanese variety.

**shallot** also called french shallots, golden shallots or eschalots.

**silver beet** also known as swiss chard and, incorrectly, spinach.

**spice, mixed** a blend of ground spices usually consisting of allspice, cinnamon and nutmeg.

**spinach** also known as english spinach and, incorrectly, silver beet.

**split peas** also known as field peas; green or yellow pulse grown especially for drying; split in half along centre.

**star anise** a dried star-shaped pod whose seeds have an astringent aniseed flavour.

**sugar**
**brown** an extremely soft, fine granulated sugar.
**caster** also known as superfine or finely granulated table sugar.
**icing** also known as confectioners' sugar or powdered sugar.
**palm** also known as nam tan pip, jaggery, jawa or gula melaka; made from the sap of the sugar palm tree. Light brown to black in colour and usually sold in rock-hard cakes; use brown sugar if palm sugar unavailable.
**raw** natural brown granulated sugar.
**white** coarse, granulated table sugar also known as crystal sugar.

**sultanas** dried grapes, also known as golden raisins.

**sumac** a purple-red, astringent spice; adds a tart, lemony flavour to recipes. Found in Middle Eastern food stores.

**sweetened condensed milk** from which 60% of the water has been removed; the remaining milk is then sweetened with sugar.

**tahini** sesame seed paste available from Middle Eastern food shops and health food stores.

**treacle** thick, dark syrup.

**turkish bread** also known as pide; comes in long (about 45cm) flat loaves as well as individual rounds.

**turmeric** also known as kamin; must be grated or pounded to release its somewhat acrid aroma and pungent flavour.

**vietnamese mint** not a mint at all, but a pungent, peppery narrow-leafed member of the buckwheat family. Available from Asian food stores.

**yeast** a 7g (¼oz) sachet of dried yeast (2 teaspoons) is equal to 15g (½oz) compressed yeast.

**zucchini** also known as courgette.

# index

# conversion guide

## measures

One Australian metric measuring cup holds approximately 250ml, one Australian metric tablespoon holds 20ml, one Australian metric teaspoon holds 5ml.

The difference between one country's measuring cups and another's is within a two- or three-teaspoon variance, and will not affect your cooking results. North America, New Zealand and the United Kingdom use a 15ml tablespoon.

All cup and spoon measurements are level. The most accurate way of measuring dry ingredients is to weigh them. When measuring liquids, use a clear glass or plastic jug with the metric markings.

We use large eggs with an average weight of 60g.

## dry measures

| metric | imperial |
| --- | --- |
| 15g | ½oz |
| 30g | 1oz |
| 60g | 2oz |
| 90g | 3oz |
| 125g | 4oz (¼lb) |
| 155g | 5oz |
| 185g | 6oz |
| 220g | 7oz |
| 250g | 8oz (½lb) |
| 280g | 9oz |
| 315g | 10oz |
| 345g | 11oz |
| 375g | 12oz (¾lb) |
| 410g | 13oz |
| 440g | 14oz |
| 470g | 15oz |
| 500g | 16oz (1lb) |
| 750g | 24oz (1½lb) |
| 1kg | 32oz (2lb) |

## liquid measures

| metric | imperial |
| --- | --- |
| 30ml | 1 fluid oz |
| 60ml | 2 fluid oz |
| 100ml | 3 fluid oz |
| 125ml | 4 fluid oz |
| 150ml | 5 fluid oz (¼ pint/1 gill) |
| 190ml | 6 fluid oz |
| 250ml | 8 fluid oz |
| 300ml | 10 fluid oz (½ pint) |
| 500ml | 16 fluid oz |
| 600ml | 20 fluid oz (1 pint) |
| 1000ml (1 litre) | 1¾ pints |

## length measures

| metric | imperial |
| --- | --- |
| 3mm | ⅛in |
| 6mm | ¼in |
| 1cm | ½in |
| 2cm | ¾in |
| 2.5cm | 1in |
| 5cm | 2in |
| 6cm | 2½in |
| 8cm | 3in |
| 10cm | 4in |
| 13cm | 5in |
| 15cm | 6in |
| 18cm | 7in |
| 20cm | 8in |
| 23cm | 9in |
| 25cm | 10in |
| 28cm | 11in |
| 30cm | 12in (1ft) |

## oven temperatures

These oven temperatures are only a guide for conventional ovens. For fan-forced ovens, check the manufacturer's manual.

| | °C (Celsius) | °F (Fahrenheit) | Gas Mark |
| --- | --- | --- | --- |
| Very slow | 120 | 250 | ½ |
| Slow | 150 | 275-300 | 1-2 |
| Moderately slow | 170 | 325 | 3 |
| Moderate | 180 | 350-375 | 4-5 |
| Moderately hot | 200 | 400 | 6 |
| Hot | 220 | 425-450 | 7-8 |
| Very hot | 240 | 475 | 9 |

Senior editor Wendy Bryant
Designer Caryl Wiggins
Food editor Louise Patniotis
Researcher Elizabeth Hooper
Food director Pamela Clark
Special feature photographer Rob Palmer
Black and white photographer Paul Suesse
Special feature stylist Stephanie Souvlis
Special feature food preparation Elizabeth Macri

ACP Books
Editorial director Susan Tomnay
Creative director Hieu Chi Nguyen
Director of sales Brian Cearnes
Marketing director Matt Dominello
Brand manager Renée Crea
Production manager Cedric Taylor
Chief executive officer John Alexander
Group publisher Pat Ingram
Publisher Sue Wannan
General manager Christine Whiston
Editorial director (WW) Deborah Thomas

WW food team Lyndey Milan, Alexandra Elliott, Frances Abdallaoui

Produced by ACP books, Sydney.
Printed by Toppan Printing, Hong Kong.
Published by ACP Magazines Ltd, 54 Park St, Sydney;
GPO Box 4088, Sydney, NSW 1028. Ph: (02) 9282 8618
Fax: (02) 9267 9438.
www.acpbooks.com.au
acpbooks@acpmagazines.com.au
To order books phone 136 116.
Send recipe enquiries to reccipeenquiries@acpmagazines.com.au
RIGHTS ENQUIRIES
Laura Bamford, Director ACP Books.
lbamford@acpmedia.co.uk

AUSTRALIA: Distributed by Network Services,GPO Box 4088, Sydney,
NSW 1028. Ph: (02) 9282 8777 Fax: (02) 9264 3278.
networkweb@networkservicescompany.com.au
UNITED KINGDOM: Distributed by Australian Consolidated Press
(UK), Moulton Park Business Centre, Red House Rd, Moulton Park,
Northampton, NN3 6AQ
Ph: (01604) 497 531 Fax: (01604) 497 533 books@acpmedia.co.uk
CANADA: Distributed by Whitecap Books Ltd, 351 Lynn Ave,
North Vancouver, BC, V7J 2C4
Ph: (604) 980 9852 Fax: (604) 980 8197
customerservice@whitecap.ca www.whitecap.ca
NEW ZEALAND: Southern Publishers Group, 44 New North Rd,
Eden Terrace, Auckland.
Ph: (64 9) 309 6930 Fax: (64 9) 309 6170 hub@spg.co.nz
SOUTH AFRICA: Distributed by PSD Promotions (Pty) Ltd, PO Box 1175,
Isando, 1600, Gauteng, Johannesburg, SA.
Ph: (011) 392 6065 Fax (011) 392 6079 orders@psdprom.co.za

Clark, Pamela.
The Australian Women's Weekly Food We Love
Includes index.
ISBN 1 86396 477 0.
1. Cookery. I.Title. II.Title: Australian Women's Weekly.

641.5
© ACP Magazines Ltd 2006
ABN 18 053 273 546

The publishers would like to thank the following for props used in
photography Major and Tom; Country Road; Plenty Homewares; Wheel
and Barrow; No Chintz for fabrics; Villeroy and Boch.

Cover Bavette with prawns, peas, lemon and dill, page 104
Photographer Brett Stevens
Stylist Marie Helene Clauzon
Back cover Quince jelly, page 216
Photographer Rob Palmer
Stylist Stephanie Souvlis

Photographers Alan Benson, Andre Martin, Andrew Young, Ben Dearnley,
Gerry Colley, Louise Lister, Ian Wallace, Joe Filshie, Rowan Fotheringham,
Steve Brown, Stuart Scott, Brett Stevens
Stylists Amber Keller, Jane Hann, Janelle Bloom, Julz Beresford, Kate Brown,
Kay Francis, Kirsty Cassidy, Louise Pickford, Marie-Helene Clauzon, Mary Harris,
Myles Beaufort, Opel Khan, Sarah O'Brien, Wendy Berecry